52 brilliantideas

KT-226-421

Create your dream garden

Tips and techniques to make
your garden bloom

Jem Cook, Anna Marsden OBE
& Mark Hillsdon

Copyright © The Infinite Ideas Company Limited, 2005

The right of Jem Cook, Mark Hillsdon and Anna Marsden to be identified as the authors of this book has been asserted in accordance with the Copyright, Designs and Patents Act 1988

First published in 2005 by
The Infinite Ideas Company Limited
36 St Giles
Oxford OX1 3LD
United Kingdom
T: 01865 514 888
E: info@infideas.com
W: www.infideas.com

All rights reserved. Except for the quotation of small passages for the purposes of criticism and review, no part of this publication may be reproduced, stored in a retrieval system or transmitted in any form or by any means, electronic, mechanical, photocopying, recording, scanning or otherwise, except under the terms of the Copyright, Designs and Patents Act 1988 or under the terms of a licence issued by the Copyright Licensing Agency Ltd, 90 Tottenham Court Road, London W1T 4LP, UK, without the permission in writing of the publisher. Requests to the publisher should be addressed to the Permissions Department, Infinite Ideas Limited, 36 St Giles, Oxford OX1 3LD, UK.

CIP catalogue records for this book are available from the British Library and the US Library of Congress.

ISBN 1-904902-24-3

Brand and product names are trademarks or registered trademarks of their respective owners.

Designed and typeset by Baseline Arts Ltd, Oxford
Printed and bound by TJ International, Cornwall

Create your dream garden

Brilliant ideas

Brilliant features

Each chapter of this book is designed to provide you with an inspirational idea that you can read quickly and put into practice straight away.

Throughout you'll find four features that will help you to get right to the heart of the idea:

- *Here's an idea for you* … Take it on board and give it a go – right here, right now. Get an idea of how well you're doing so far.

- *Try another idea* … If this idea looks like a life-changer then there's no time to lose. *Try another idea* … will point you straight to a related tip to enhance and expand on the first.

- *Defining ideas* Words of wisdom from masters and mistresses of the art, plus some interesting hangers-on.

- *How did it go?* If at first you do succeed try to hide your amazement. If, on the other hand, you don't, then this is where you'll find a Q and A that highlights common problems and how to get over them.

Introduction

OK, so you know one end of a spade from another, vaguely remember something your Grandma told you about deadheading roses, and love the idea of a pond in your garden, just like the one you saw on the telly.

Your garden intrigues you, yet scares you at the same time. You love the idea of growing your own vegetables but worry about using chemicals to keep the pests off. And as much as you love them, why exactly do some clematis insist on having their roots in the shade?

Starting any new hobby – and let's face it, to most of us that's exactly what gardening is – can be a steep learning curve. And as you gaze out of the back door and realise you can only confidently name half a dozen of the plants growing away in your borders, it can be a struggle to know where to start.

Take heart. You just need to follow a few simple rules, keep an open mind about learning new things and, most importantly, be realistic about what you can achieve in the spare time you have. Plants do grow, and often with the minimum of fuss and effort if you get a few basics right.

It used to be that gardening was something you took up in retirement, muddling through with a few evergreens until you hit sixty, when an overwhelming urge to grow everything in shades of pink takes over. Not so today, as the boom of interest in growing things and 'living' in the garden has spawned a new generation of gardeners keen to replicate what they see on the telly.

The joy of gardening is not just the huge array of plants you can propagate, pamper and prune, but that there are so many different levels at which to do it. It could be as simple as scattering a few seeds or planting up a window box, or as complex as planning an orchard or growing something exotic.

Gardening can also be a microcosm of life, full of successes and failures, packed with highs and lows. It can also be a chance to get fit, develop your creative skills and get closer to wildlife.

Throughout the book there is an unapologetic bias towards organic gardening. We believe it's the best way to tend your plot, working with nature rather than against her, encouraging nature to keep the balance, not chemicals. But you'll be glad to know we don't just pontificate and leave things there. From dealing with common diseases to creating your own compost, this book is a checklist for how to garden organically.

It's also big on getting the basics rights. Do that, and the rest will follow. Good soil, regular watering, plants in the right place, the correct way to prune – it may sound a bit daunting, but it really does become clear with practice. And if you do get it wrong, you'll know what not to do next time.

Some of the chapters will give just a taste of what can be achieved, whetting your appetite for finding out more. Others are our take on old favourites like pergolas, plums and pansies. Oh, and there's also a bit about gnomes too.

As well as fruit and veg there are ideas about how to get the best from some of our most popular flowers and shrubs, and how to achieve that horticultural nirvana, year-round interest.

Every gardener needs a project, and we've come up with a few ideas that should keep you busy, from building structures with local, recycled materials, to digging a pond and choosing a greenhouse.

But ultimately, everything links back to your soil. Improve the soil and you'll improve the chances of your plants reaching their true potential.

What you won't find in this book is a crash course in garden design, a quick fix to the perfect garden makeover. Of course not everyone can spend as long in the garden as they would like. We all have other demands on our time. The answer is to accept that a garden is an evolving thing and that, although there are certain times when it's best to do specific tasks, it's largely forgiving and there's always next year.

Next time you pull on your gardening gloves and reach for your secateurs, remember the words of that gardening doyenne Gertrude Jekyll: 'There is not a spot of ground, however arid, bare or ugly, that cannot be tamed.' Just make sure you tame it organically.

Jem Cook, Mark Hillsdon and Anna Marsden

1

Did the earth move?

Not knowing what sort of soil you have in your garden is like guessing between sugar and salt in the kitchen – a recipe for disaster.

Hands up who knows what pH stands for? No, we didn't have a clue either but apparently it's vital to how your garden grows.

The old saying *'the answer lies in the soil'* is invariably true. Get to know your soil and you can add the right stuff to improve it, and grow the types of plants that will enjoy it. Hardly anyone gardens on rich, light loam but each soil type still has its own distinct merits.

THE ACID TEST

To find the pH (read on, dear reader, read on) of your soil you need a soil-testing kit, available at any garden centre. This will help you find out what kind of soil you're gardening on. And with this small yet vital snippet of information, you'll know how to feed your soil and what plants you can grow.

It pays to take three or four samples from the outer edges of the garden as you may have more than one soil type, each favouring different plants and treatments. The test will show whether your samples are acidic (below 7), neutral (7) or alkaline (above 7).

Here's an
idea for
you...

Raised beds may be a solution if you have particularly difficult soil and want to grow a range of vegetables and herbs. Build them approx 1.5m square so they can be worked from the sides without standing on the soil. Edge the beds, to a height of 30cm or more, to keep the soil in place. Use old railway sleepers, woven hazel, reclaimed bricks, galvanised steel, whatever takes your fancy. Fork over the soil to improve the drainage and then dig in as much compost as possible, adding a fresh layer of compost each time you replant.

Most garden plants favour soil that is slightly acidic at 6.5, but there's still a good selection of plants for neutral and alkaline soils.

With your pH sorted, discovering your soil type is even easier. Just pick some up. If it's tightly packed, squeezes into a sticky ball and hangs about on your boots – it's clay. If it feels gritty, and water runs through it easily – it's sandy. If you discover the white cliffs of Dover under the surface – it's chalk.

Clay soil is hard to work. It's wet and cloggy in winter and bakes rock hard in a dry spell. But it is full of good things and the nutrients your plants need to grow, so don't despair. You do need to improve its drainage though, so mix in some horticultural grit or coarse sand when planting. Clay soil is usually neutral to acidic too so add lime – ground down calcium – especially if you're growing brassicas. Turn unplanted ground over in the autumn and leave the frost to break up the big lumps.

Dig in or spread as much compost as you can, whenever the conditions suit. Timing is crucial but it's the soil and the weather that set the time, not you! As soon as it's dry enough to stand on without it turning into a mud bath, get to work.

Defining
idea...

'Soil is rather like a lucky dip – you only get out of it what you put in!'
Traditional saying

Success on sand will depend on how you can help the soil hang on to food and moisture.

Adding in compost will help retain water and fertiliser long enough for it to do some good. But this will need to become a regular chore so you may wish to just focus on parts of the garden where you are growing hungry, thirsty plants such as the veg.

Compost, compost, compost! Having mentioned it so many times you'd better turn to IDEA 7, *Sweet smelling brown stuff*.

Try another idea...

Because any fertiliser will pass through the soil quickly, spread it a little and often. Sandy soil can be acidic and will benefit from a light application of lime (250g per square metre – half that for clay soils). A bonus is that the soil is easy to work on and quick to warm up in spring, so grow early crops that will mature before things get too dry.

Chalky soil can be stony, or sticky and thin, but it's well-drained and you can work on it most of the year. Bulk it up by adding organic matter. Horse manure, which tends to be full of straw, is good for sticky chalk. As it breaks down relatively quickly, spread it on the surface and leave the earthworms to do their bit. Dig in any left-over straw in the spring.

Remember, chalky soil is alkaline and certain plants won't like it a bit. You can give plants a helping hand at the start of the growing season by sprinkling in bonemeal or blood, fish and bone, to compensate for the lack of phosphate and to help roots develop.

'The health of the soil, plant, animal and man is one and indivisible'
LADY EVE BALFOUR, founder of the Organic Soil Association

Defining idea...

Just to recap, most plants like clay soils, drought tolerant plants are for sandy soils and plant lime-lovers on chalk. This means that azaleas, camellias, rhododendrons and heathers (except the winter flowering *Erica carnea*) will not grow on chalk but plenty of other plants, and most herbs, love it.

Oh and pH, that'll be potential hydrogen. Nope, we're none the clearer either.

Q   Can I dig out some of my chalky soil and replace it with more acidic compost to grow some camellias?

A   *You can, but acid loving shrubs (camellias, rhododendrons and azaleas) might look odd amongst a garden of chalk loving plants. It would be better to plant your camellia as a freestanding specimen in a pot, where it can be admired in all its splendour without looking out of place. And enjoy azaleas by visiting gardens where they flourish.*

Q   My beautiful blue hydrangea has turned pink. Is this because of my soil?

A   *Blue hydrangeas are a sure sign of acid soil. If your soil is neutral a regular iron tonic should help recover its blue rinse. Some suggest burying nails around the plant but modern nails often aren't rusty enough!*

Q   Any suggestions for dry, sandy beds?

A   *Plants that cope well in dry conditions often have narrow or furry silver/grey leaves. Succulents and many grasses do well. Try Artemisia, Verbascum, Cistus, lavender, Eryngium, Senecio cineraria and wisteria.*

2

Top seed

Every seed is a gardening miracle, a small, dried-out husk that a few months after planting bursts into flower and brings new life to the garden.

At least this is what it seems like when they actually sprout. But of course, as with everything in the garden, there's a flip side, and the euphoria of a growing seedling is easily dampened by the sight of a tiny shrivelled stem, or bare patch of earth that once promised so much.

Whether you've harvested your own or bought a packet, sowing them indoors can certainly give them a head start, as you've much more control, not just over the temperature but also over the pests that will chew off a shoot quicker than you can say slug pellets.

The first rule of successful sowing is to read the packet! It should tell you all you need to know. For instance, do your seeds need soaking before you plant them? This can soften the outer husks or remove chemicals that prevent them from

Here's an idea for you...

Growing from seed is an excellent way of raising unusual plants that you can't always buy in a mature state. You can also select your own colour combinations rather than put up with those more commonly available.

Defining idea...

'One of the healthiest ways to gamble is with a spade and a package of garden seeds.'
DAN BENNETT

Defining idea...

'Seedsmen reckon that their stock in trade is not seeds at all ... it's optimism.'
GEOFF HAMILTON

germinating. Are they suitable for sowing in trays or pots, or should you sow them directly into the ground?

Cleanliness is, of course, next to godliness, and while scrubbing out seed trays with hot soapy water is akin to rubbing down paintwork before you open your tin of gloss, it's still a crucial if somewhat laborious task.

While the professionals use all kinds of weird and wonderful 'growing' mediums such as rock-wool, a good-quality seed compost is probably best for the amateur. Try to get one that contains sterilised loam and a peat substitute, which will be finer and more moisture retentive than either a general-purpose compost or home-grown humus, which will be too rich for the seeds.

Making sure the compost is firmed down is also important. This helps to avoid any subterranean air pockets which, just as it looks like the seedlings are taking hold, can cause sudden subsidence with the whole lot suddenly disappearing down a gaping chasm.

Bear in mind too that some seeds such as Canterbury Bells (*Campanula medium*) need light to germinate so sow them on the surface.

As a rule of thumb, the larger the seed the easier it is to grow. Big buggers like lupins and sweet peas are best sown individually in pots, which means they can develop a good strong root system before you disturb them and plant them out. Or better still in this environmentally conscious age, why not use a biodegradable pot. Used for larger seeds, you can miss out the pricking out stage and just plant the whole thing, pot 'n all, into the ground.

If the thriftiness of getting something for nothing appeals, then check out IDEA 4, *Don't pay the nurseryman*, for more tips on stocking your garden for free.

Try another idea...

Unless you particularly enjoy surprises you need to be disciplined when it comes to labelling, and as soon as you've finished one pot or tray, get it labelled or you'll spend the next few weeks wondering …

'A good gardener always plants three seeds – one for the bugs, one for the weather and one for himself.'
LEO AIKMAN

Defining idea...

If you have a greenhouse, or a heated propagator, then lucky you. For the rest of us it's time to reclaim those window sills with homemade propagators using clear plastic bags, sticks and a seed tray.

If you have a propagator remember to use square pots simply because round ones waste valuable space.

'Think of the fierce energy concentrated in an acorn! You bury it in the ground, and it explodes into an oak! Bury a sheep, and nothing happens but decay.'
GEORGE BERNARD SHAW

Defining idea...

As they develop, your seeds will need differing levels of light, warmth, air and moisture and, once that shoot appears, nutrients as well. Read up on what you have to do so that you aren't caught on the hop.

As a general rule, the trick is to make sure the compost is damp but not waterlogged; the atmosphere is humid but not dripping. A watering can with a fine rose will help and you can improve the overall drainage by part filling the bottom of the pots with gravel.

Next you need to prick them out by gently prising out each seedling by its leaves (not the stalk) using a dibber, and move it on to a pot of its own, before growing them on, hardening them off, and planting them out. Then you can enjoy them. Nobody said it was going to be easy!

How did it go?

Q   My seedlings have just shrivelled and died. Why?

A   *Sounds like damping off, which is caused by a fungi that thrives in moist, warm conditions. It can be caused by too many seedlings too close together, and too much water, which makes them rot on the surface.*

Q   How do I know if the seeds I've collected are viable?

A   *The best way to test them is to put them in a jar of water. Those that are dead float, those that are viable sink.*

Q   Success! My seedlings have germinated but now they won't stop growing and are starting to flop over. How come?

A   *While you should always keep seedlings in a light, airy place, this can cause them to get leggy. With a bit of luck though, if you plant them deeply enough when you prick them out, so that a good portion of the stem is under the surface, they should pull though.*

3

Doing yer nut

A nut tree in your garden? You must admit it's an enticing proposition, but how do you go about wetting your walnuts and harvesting your hazels, without providing a free feast for Squirrel Nutkin and his chums?

The British Isles is not exactly famed for its nuts. For decades the hazelnut, which has nuts that stay fresh for several months, was a mainstay of the Navy, and its close relative the cobnut was once a popular crop down in Kent. But many of the great walnuts that once graced our parks and gardens were plundered during the Napoleonic Wars, when walnut became the musket makers' wood of choice.

Other factors such as their size, slow growth rate and the fact they are fussy pollinators have also seen the nut tree decline as a garden tree, but new varieties and growing methods could see their stock rise again.

Here's an idea for you... **Here's a project that should keep you interested for years to come! To grow sweet chestnuts, collect plump, ripe healthy-looking nuts in autumn. Remove the spiky casings and then float them in water. Only the nuts that sink are viable, so pot them up immediately but give them some protection from both frost and the squirrels.**

NUT CASE

Traditionally grown in an orchard or 'plat' the cobnut is probably the easiest nut tree to grow. It's also frost tolerant to a degree, although it won't withstand a heavy hoar. Multi-stemmed and smaller than the walnut, the best yielding trees are pruned back to around 1.8m (6ft) between winter and spring.

Crucially cobnuts must be planted in pairs to encourage cross pollination. If you live in the countryside with indigenous hazel nearby, that should be enough to do the job, otherwise you will need to plant two different varieties. Recommended cultivars include the Kentish Cob and Gunselbert, and nurseries will be able to tell you if a variety needs a specific pollinator (some varieties, such as the Kentish Cob, are biennial).

The trees prefer sun or light shade, with their roots in a poor to moderately fertile soil. And while feeding isn't needed, certain varieties do relish a good hard pruning. The cobnut is also a favourite with wildlife and may entice nuthatches and even dormice to your garden.

VENEER OF RESPECTABILITY

Not for the walnut any minimalist chic or waif-like posturing; the walnut is a real tree. Handsome, noble, majestic, these are the words that describe this tree, with a stout and sturdy trunk which supports a broad spreading crown of mid-green leaves, festooned with catkins in the spring and rich in nuts during the autumn.

As a seedling, a walnut can take up to 15 years to fruit, but grafted to root stock, will usually crop in three. Getting them through the first few years is the tricky bit. The key is to plant them in deep, fertile soil, in a sheltered place with as much sun as possible. They also love nitrogen so no skimping on the manure.

Unlike cobnuts, some varieties of walnut are self fertile, including both Broadview and Buccaneer, while others need a partner to ensure cross pollination.

As for yield, the new cultivars are better croppers than traditional varieties, and from the last week of August you can get picking.

BITTER SWEET

For the ambitious, an altogether trickier proposition is growing a sweet almond, which can grow up to about 6.7m (22ft), with delicate pink or white flowers that bloom in early spring appearing before the long serrated leaves. The trees can be trained up a wall or left to become thick and bushy, and cross pollination is essential.

IDEA 43, *Small trees for small gardens* goes into more detail about how to choose and plant trees. And for other fruiting trees, IDEA 17, *Oranges are not the only fruit*, tickles the taste buds with some pointers about apple and pear trees.

Try another idea...

'I got to wondering where they [the squirrels] are putting most of the [wal]nuts. It would obviously be close to the trees they collect from and in softer soil rather then harder. So I started building up leaves and mulches underneath the trees, making it softer and deeper.
  'Now I happily let the squirrels bury the nuts. I come along and rake vigorously and deeply, working outwards from the base of each tree and soon unearth enough for me.'
BOB FLOWERDEW

Defining idea...

Originally from the Mediterranean, frost and almonds don't mix, but they can be grown in a conservatory. Outside, the best spot is a sunny, south-facing wall, with well-drained and loamy soil. Containerising any stone fruits isn't easy, and watering is crucial. Cultivars such as Ferradual come grafted to root stock, and will crop in four to five years.

As well as delicious fruit, the other great boon of nut trees is that with the exception of a touch of peach leaf curl on almonds, they are largely disease resistant.

How did it go?

Q   I'm at my wits end with squirrels! What can I do?

A   *Public enemy number one with nut growers is the grey squirrel. Their introduction into Britain at the end of the 1800s had a devastating effect on nut harvests, and even a lone squirrel can strip a hazel quicker than you can say cross pollination. Short of trapping or shooting, one way of protecting cobnuts is to hard prune so you can actually house them in a steel fruit cage. Alternatively, certain brands of animal deterrents keep the critters at bay. For walnuts beat the squirrels by picking the nuts before they are ripe and then pickle them.*

Q   I've heard that the walnut sap is toxic. Is that correct?

A   *True, it acts as a natural weedkiller, so it's worth remembering that few plants are hardy enough to grow underneath a walnut tree. And instead of composting any leaves and clippings, burn them first and then add the nutrient-rich ash to the compost heap.*

4

Don't pay the nurseryman

From dividing to layering, taking cuttings to swapping with friends – here's how to stock your garden for free.

It's extraordinary how many ways there are to make your own plants. Some methods are simple, others involve a little technical know-how and a bit of practice. But let's face it, we all like getting something for free, so clear some space in the greenhouse and get to grips with the art of propagation.

LONG DIVISION

Forget the calculator, this division involves a little bit of persuasion, and a pair of garden forks. Perennials can be teased apart to form three or more smaller plants.

Simply dig up dense clumps of border plants and insert two forks, back to back, into the middle of the clump. Lever the forks back and forth and the plant should give way and separate. The oldest, middle bit is best thrown away, as it's the younger,

Here's an idea for you...

There are several ways to increase your chances of success with your cuttings:

- **When taking a cutting put it into a plastic bag until ready to use.**
- **Try dipping semi-ripe or hardwood cuttings into rooting powder to get them started – tap off excess and don't return used powder to the pot.**
- **Place cuttings around the edge of the pot – this seems to work best although there is no scientific evidence!**
- **Label all cuttings.**
- **Always add grit or sharp sand to the compost to ensure it drains well.**

more vigorous outer growth that will yield new plants. Make sure you plant them straight away.

Clumps of hostas, more than a few years old, can be sliced through with a sharp spade.

CUTTINGS

Having conquered division we're onto multiplication. Cuttings can be taken from soft, semi-ripe or hard wood, as well as from the roots and leaves, all at different times of the year. Different plants respond to different methods so a bit of reading up is required but here are some general rules:

- Soft wood cuttings (taken from the top of the stem) work for perennials and most shrubs, and should be taken in spring. The cutting needs to be up to 7cm long. Cut just below a leaf node (the bit where the leaves form) and remove the lower leaves. Root these cuttings first in a jar of water and move to small pots of compost once the roots have formed.

- Semi-ripe cuttings (using wood that is soft at the top and firmer at the base) for trees shrubs and roses, should be taken in mid-to-late summer. Ease a shoot, about 12cm long, from the plant so that a 'heel' of the parent plant remains attached. Leave the top foliage on and put the bare part into the compost. Place several cuttings into one pot, moving each onto individual pots once a good root has formed.

- Hard wood (strong, hard stems from the current year's growth, with soft top removed) for shrubs and some fruits, taken between mid-autumn and early winter. Take pencil thick cuttings, trim to 20cm long, making a straight cut at the bottom, just below a leaf node, and a slanted cut at the top, above a leaf node. Place cuttings in an outside trench or potted in a cold frame and leave for up to a year.

- Root cuttings, taken from the roots of trees shrubs or herbaceous plants, should be taken when the plant is dormant in the autumn. Unearth some of the root and remove a piece about the width of a pencil and as long as possible. Cut this into pieces of at least 5cm. To ensure you plant them the right way up, cut the end that was severed from the plant straight, the other end at an angle. Place them in a pot with the straight end showing just above the surface, cover with 1cm of sharp sand and leave out until the spring

- Leaf cuttings, from healthy fully developed leaves, work especially well with begonias and African violets. Either carefully remove

IDEA 2, *Top Seed*, looks at ways to ensure your seeds do exactly what they should.

Try another idea...

'If you take cuttings of tender plants before spring arrives, it will make all the difference to the summer show. Pot them on frequently and not only will they produce big buxom plants but there will also be time to take further cuttings to swell the ranks in the same year.'
CAROL KLEIN

Defining idea...

15

the whole leaf, complete with stalk, and inset into a shallow hole in a pot of compost, or nick the underside veins of a leaf and lay it topside up on the compost surface. Cut sword-like leaves into sections of 5cm long and insert each upright into the compost. Once plantlets develop pot them on.

Layering sometimes takes place naturally, when a branch from a shrub or climber roots in the soil while it's still attached to the plant.

You can give nature a helping hand by selecting a flexible stem, bending it to the ground, nicking the underside and pegging it in place with a staple (bent wire or wooden peg). Cover with soil. Once a good root has formed, sever the stem from the parent plant and pot it up.

Budding and grafting is challenging stuff. Ask an expert to show you how or enrol on a short Royal Horticultural Society (RHS) or adult education course.

While it's only natural to try and save money and do it yourself, we should of course remember that good nurseries are needed to supply fine plants in the first place, so it's well worth supporting them where you can.

Q **I got lucky with my cuttings and now have too many to cope with. Lobbing them on the compost heap seems so brutal! What's the alternative?**

How did it go?

A *Why not share your success with your friends and neighbours, offering them the spare plants? If you have friends who also propagate their own plants, get together and decide who's growing what, so there is no duplication or waste. Sometimes whole communities get organised and hold 'Plant Swap Days'.*

Q **When my mother-in-law saw my withered seedlings she said I obviously hadn't heard of hardening off. I hadn't ... Should I have?**

A *Once a plant – either grown from seed or a cutting – has plenty of roots and shoots, and is ready for planting out, it will need to gradually get used to the outside temperature, especially at night. This is known as hardening off and can be achieved by placing the pot in a cold frame, leaving the lid open at night after the first few days. If you don't have a cold frame, place the pots in a sheltered spot against the house and bring them in at night if a frost threatens.*

5

Indian summer

Why let your borders flop at the end of July when with a bit of TLC and a sharp pair of secateurs you could be enjoying a second show of colour?

It stands to reason that you want to get as colourful and as long-lasting a display as possible from your flowers, especially given the effort that's gone into getting them to bloom in the first place.

Clipping plants back after flowering can seem drastic but in a week or two fresh leaves will provide the perfect foil for other plants yet to perform.

CRUEL TO BE KIND

The lungwort (*Pulmonaria*) is one of those harbingers of spring that gives you faith in the new season to come. Its blue and pink flowers (there are varieties that have just blue or white flowers too) are a welcome supply of nectar for early bees, but when they've done their bit be ruthless, and cut them off, together with most of the leaves. Water well and feed with a handful of bonemeal, and fresh dappled leaves with their 'spilt milk' markings) will soon appear.

Here's an idea for you... **Once they've flowered, shrubs and climbing roses could do with a bit of a lift. Plant the freely wandering, late flowering *Clematis tangutica* or some colourful climbing nasturtiums to ramble through and brighten things up.**

You can be equally brutal with poppies (*Papaver orientale*) and also Lady's mantle (*Alchemilla molis*), once its lime green flowers show the first sign of browning (this will also prevent self-seeding, which this plant is particularly keen on). Hold back with the secateurs, and the leaves of these early performers will fade, rust and crumple by midsummer.

Plants that start flowering in the early summer can also benefit from a haircut to encourage a second flush of colour. Cat mint (*Nepeta*) and the pink flowering geranium (*endressii*) are two useful front-of-the-border fillers that respond well to this treatment. And if you cut them back just half at a time, you keep a succession of flowers and prevent the pudding-basin haircut appearance.

If you cut centaurea, delphiniums, anthemis and salvias back to ground level after flowering they may surprise you with a second flush too.

REGULAR SERVICING

Midsummer is the time when you can really get to know and enjoy your plants, learning things about them that you can put into practice next year. There are often no big or laborious jobs that need doing – this is the time to potter. A bit of deadheading, a touch of cutting back and your border will keep its shape for weeks to come.

Deadhead once a week if possible – unless you want seeds for next year. Cutting off the spent flowers helps the plant put its energy into flowering again, instead of producing unwanted seeds.

When plants begin to look sad and need cutting right back, gaps may start to appear which can spoil the overall effect. While neighbouring plants may spread into the space, you can also strategically place the odd pot or container, submerging them out of sight. Alternatively, use some late flowering annuals, such as cosmos or lavatera. And, if you're organised, now's the time to send in the reinforcements, those spare plants grown from seed that you couldn't squeeze in early in the year but can now get in amongst them and play their part.

The real key to prolonging the border's display is succession planting. With a bit of thought and a season or two's experience, you'll soon become a dab hand. Try to think ahead. Group your plants together so that they not only complement each other in colour, height and leaf shape but also in flowering season. This simply means including some later flowering perennials close to your early performers.

Especially useful from midsummer until the first frosts are the Michaelmas daisy (*Aster*) and other daisy flowers (*Rudbeckia, Helenium, Echinacea*), the thistle-like *Eryngium* and *Echinops*, Japanese anemone and dahlias. Intersperse these next to plants that are in bloom in spring and you'll have a blooming border right through to late autumn.

Staking your plants well but discreetly is important to maintain the shape of your border. IDEA 10, *Support network*, will take you through this.

Try another idea...

'Around mid-July, another change starts to come over the garden as the early cast of summer shrubs and perennials dies away... Presenting this next wave of shrubs and perennials well means maintaining some sense of order and design amid the burgeoning growth. Serious sessions with shears and strimmers are de rigueur, and work wonders. I am like a gunfighter with my left-handed secateurs, whipping them out of their holster at the slightest provocation.'
STEPHEN LACEY, in *Real Gardening*

Defining idea...

Q   My dahlias look fantastic from midsummer onwards but looking after them sounds such a pain. Is it as bad as it sounds?

A   *True there is more to dahlias than just cutting them back, unless you live in a very mild area, where you could try leaving them in place, cutting them down, and covering them with protective mulch. Otherwise you need to lift and store the tubers. The key to it is keeping them dry and protected from frost.*

Dig up the dahlias once the foliage has been blackened by the first frost, leaving on about 10–15cm of stalk. Gently remove as much soil as possible and put them in the garage or greenhouse to dry off. Once completely dry remove any remaining soil and find a frost-free place to store them until spring. You can put them in shredded paper to ensure they keep dry. In early spring replace the paper with compost to encourage them to start growing. Once healthy shoots and the first leaves appear, and there is no further threat of frost, plant them back in the border, putting plenty of compost in the planting hole.

Q   I've tried deadheading but get confused between newly opening buds and shrivelling flowers. How can I tell the difference?

A   *I know what you mean. It's not always easy to tell and petunias are particularly tricky. As a general rule if you can see a seed head forming in the centre of the flower it is time to snip it off. You'll soon get the hang of this, noticing too, the position on the stem of old flowers as opposed to the new ones. Persevere as the rewards are great – longer and fuller flowering.*

6

Design without the despair

You don't need a degree in landscape architecture to give shape to your garden – just a bit of inspiration and a rudimentary knowledge of elbow grease.

Starting from scratch is both daunting and exciting. You're about to invest a lot of time, and quite a few quid, into turning your weed-strewn plot into something with a little more structure, style and sophistication. So from the start it pays to have some vision or picture of how things are going to look when you're finished.

You need to get a feel for the site, thinking about what could go where and then working out whether it really should. Where are the garden's sunny spots? Where's the shade? Does anywhere tend to get waterlogged?

But at the same time don't get bogged down in detail because there's a lot to be said for seat-of-the-pants design. In other words go out and make a start. Keep standing back – even viewing from an upstairs window – and you'll soon get a feel

Here's an idea for you... **Take your inspiration from other gardens, whether big or small. And you don't necessarily have to visit Sissinghurst to glean ideas. Many villages organise garden strolls – not to mention the National Garden Scheme, which lists gardens open for charity in its famous _Yellow Book_.**

for shape and proportion. The best advice at this stage of the proceedings is to leave the tape measure in the tool box.

SETTING YOUR SITES

The first essential is to establish which direction your garden faces. On a suitable day follow the path of the sun across your garden noting the variations in light and shade, because while you may be basking in the reflected glory of a south-facing plot, it could sit under the canopy of the neighbour's spreading chestnut tree for most of the day.

Apropos neighbours, it pays to learn a little of their own gardening ambitions too. Is their newly planted leylandii to remain at a clipped 4 feet or allowed a free rein? And would neighbours on the other side mind if your clematis peeps over the top of their lapped larch fence?

Now, we all like our privacy but it's easy to become a bit obsessive about screening our gardens from the rest of the world. This is the difference between the British and Dutch gardening philosophies. We hide behind walls, fences and the densest hedges known to man, while the Dutch open their gardens for everybody to view as they pass by.

OK, now the fun really starts. Armed with small stakes or pegs mark out certain areas, such as the herbaceous border, rose bed and vegetable patch. A hosepipe is a great help in doing this. Being both light and flexible it will give you an immediate outline on which you can pass judgment.

At this stage, don't even think about any permanent structures like brick walls – their role and positioning will become more obvious as the rest of the garden takes shape. Shifting a few barrow loads of misplaced soil is one thing – reconstructing a wall or concrete path is another.

If you don't have the space for a pergola, IDEA 10, *Support network*, explains how hazel rods can be used to create temporary support structures for a variety of plants.

Try another idea...

OFF THE STRAIGHT AND NARROW

Unless you have a plot the size of Versailles, try and upset the symmetry of your garden, or at best confine any rigid formality and straight lines to the vegetable plot.

If you want a water feature, fine, but remember it doesn't have to be a lake if you only have a few square feet to play with. You could always confine yourself to a mini fountain or birdbath while the children are young and unaware of the potential dangers of a pond.

No matter how small your garden, you can still make use of existing rises and falls too, or create new and different levels. They help give the impression of more space and give you the opportunity to make a new patio or seating area.

'I uphold Beatrix Farrand's sentiment (Gertrude Jeykell's too) that the design should always fit the site; the site should not be bent to the design.'
ROSEMARY VEREY

Defining idea...

The idea should be to create mystery! Try not to open everything up at once. Add fences, a winding path, a trellis or pergola smothered in climbers, which will tempt visitors to find out what's going on behind.

And treat permanent buildings as assets too. Cover garage walls with a cotoneaster; grow a wisteria on a south facing house wall; take advantage of a porch with a climbing rose. Even log stores or coalbunkers can look aesthetically pleasing given the right treatment. Cover up manholes or drain covers with a pot.

How did it go?

Q   **You say throw the tape measure away but I have access to computer technology. Can this help me design a garden?**

A   *Certainly. Computer buffs score well here as you can create a three-dimensional picture. However, I'd only use it as a very basic guide as Mother Nature can play nasty and deceitful tricks even on the most sophisticated electronic plans.*

Q   **My original concept was to make as natural-looking a garden as possible. I have few straight lines and no symmetry yet it still looks too organised and slightly twee. Where am I going wrong?**

A   *Your gardening philosophy sounds perfect and I'm sure the effect will come as your garden matures. Let plants intermingle and drip and flow over the edges of paths. You know how French women, having spent hours in front of the mirror, achieve that look of studied dishevelment. Adopt that concept in your garden by having a plan without being too exact.*

7

Sweet smelling brown stuff

A garden without a compost heap is like a car without an engine – it ain't going anywhere.

Although there may be a tendency to get a bit self-righteous about one's compost heap, you can't really consider yourself a true gardener until you've mastered the art of turning potato peelings into black gold.

Many of us have childhood memories of a mound of dark, sweet-smelling black stuff somewhere in the garden. It was a breeding ground for small red worms that were perfect for fishing. You may also remember a chemical-ridden, toxic heap of grass cuttings that oozed a black slime and smelt like a chemical works. It's not hard to work out which one is more likely to make your roses grow.

HEAP OR HYPE?

First attempts at a compost heap can soon turn into a dumping ground for any garden waste (but never, ever dog waste). This system also means the heap might grow to a size more suited to a small National Trust property. So the first rule of composting is to know what goes on the heap and what goes on the fire.

Befriend your local greengrocer. They discard sackfuls of perfect composting material every day. If you're not already doing your ecologically friendly bit make a start here.

For starters, perennial weeds and anything diseased should be burnt, while anything too woody, unless finely shredded, should be bagged up and taken to the local tip. And only add cooked foodstuffs if you want to attract a family of rats to your garden.

Now for the good bits. Kitchen waste is perfect and if you're serious about this (which you should be) set up a separate bin for your peelings and pods, and train the family to use it.

The autumn clear up, particularly of the herbaceous borders, will also give you plenty of raw material.

Defining idea...

'A fool looks for dung where the cow never browsed.'
Ethiopian proverb

Grass cuttings are a permanent source of controversy. Use them by all means but layer them between other fibrous material, to avoid the black, nourishment-free slurry mentioned earlier.

Dead leaves can also be tricky if just dumped on a heap. But they are worth persevering with, so store them separately in punctured plastic bags or, better still, in chickenwire cages. They will compost, but in years rather than months.

The other perennial question is whether a compost heap should be wet or dry. The advice is neither. Yes, it needs to be covered with something like an old piece of carpet, as this helps build up the heat and accelerates decomposition. But it pays to leave it exposed occasionally to rain, as it shouldn't be allowed to dry out.

One friend also regularly adds his own urine, although whether he's on a mission to boost its nitrogen content, or just too lazy to go to the upstairs loo, is another question completely.

IDEA 8, *Tools of the trade*, deals with self-mulching grass cutters.

Try another idea...

The ultimate prize is horse or cow manure, and you'll be surprised how easy it is to get hold of the stuff, even if you live in town, with it's riding schools and city farms. However, don't be tempted to spread fresh manure as this will scorch your plants. Leave it for at least six months, until it no longer resembles dung and is more like crumbly soil.

In an ideal world you need three bins. Leave a full bin for approximately three months before turning it into the next one. Then repeat the process and you should achieve the ultimate crumbly brown compost within six to nine months.

'Earth knows no desolation. She smells regeneration in the moist breath of decay.'
GEORGE MEREDITH (novelist)

Defining idea...

There are two schools of thought as to the best time to spread it, either late autumn or early spring. In spring the compost has had that bit longer to reach a state of readiness, and the ground is at its hungriest. But spreading in the late autumn is fine as well, as long as you don't cover frozen ground.

Compost can be used to regenerate poor soil, helps break up heavy, clay soil and enables light soil to hold on to water and nutrients. On chalky soil use it as a mulch, spreading it on the surface for the worms to carry down. With other soils, dig it in.

'Money is like manure – it's not worth anything unless you spread it around.'
UNKNOWN

Defining idea...

The compost bins themselves play a vital role but needn't cost the earth. To construct three bins that have an air of originality, take eight 10cm × 10cm posts, 1.5m tall and either plane a groove the length of the posts or nail strips of wood to form the grooves. Having set the posts in the ground, cut planks of wood to the required length and slot them in. The rougher the wood the better – offcuts from sawmills are great, especially those showing bark as this will help them blend with their surroundings, unlike the ubiquitous green plastic bins.

The timber's irregularities also allow air into the compost to encourage the decomposing process.

How did it go?

Q **I've done it! I've made tons of fantastic compost and I've been spreading it everywhere. But I've got a lot left. What else can I do with it?**

A *When putting in new plants or moving those that are already established, line any hole with your compost. The same applies to shrubs or young trees. Before you plant sweet peas or runner beans dig a trench two spits deep (a spit is a spade-depth of earth) and line the trench with layers of sodden newspaper, which helps prevent water loss. Cover generously with compost before returning the soil.*

Q **The compost I made seems great but how come I've got more slugs than ever?**

A *Immature compost is slug friendly. They thrive on it. Make sure the compost is well rotted before spreading.*

8

Tools of the trade

From the unusual to the indispensable, here's what you'll find in all the best garden sheds this year.

Your garden shed is the bulwark of the garden, the quartermaster's stores. But what you keep in it is worth some serious thought because if there's one aspect of gardening where you mustn't skimp, this is it.

The basics haven't changed much in the tool department for years, although modern refinements in design and materials have increased efficiency and made the gardener's job a little easier. Simplicity is still key, though, and the more complex the tool the greater the chance of it breaking down.

Before deciding on which brand of tool to purchase try out a few. Borrow from family and friends, or spend time handling them in the shop. Compare several and get a feel for their weight and balance. Imagine using the tool for half an hour or more. Only you will know what feels right in your hands. Check for quality of finish and the firmness of the handles.

Here's an idea for you... **Invest in an adjustable rake. In recent years there have been few non-mechanical tools that have come onto the market that have revolutionised any aspect of gardening – but this is a notable exception. A simple lever on the back of the rake head allows you to narrow or widen the gaps between the prongs. This makes it a real all-rounder, allowing easy raking between plants in the borders or prize specimens in the shrub bed, but also strong enough to scarify the lawn in autumn, as well as gather fallen leaves.**

ACE OF SPADES

First and foremost buy the best spade on the market. It should be made of stainless steel – it's rust free, easy to clean and will slide through even the stickiest soils.

Take care too over your second in command, the garden fork. Buy a cheap one and the tines will twist or the shaft split at the first sign of hard work. Here the choice of handle and how the stem is secured to the prongs are most important. Select the size you feel comfortable with, one that will suit the jobs you have in mind – a heavy-duty fork for digging and turning the compost heap or a smaller border fork for areas full of plants.

UNUSUAL SUSPECTS

But I'm reserving pride of place for three unlikely and certainly unheralded tools: the pickaxe, the builder's barrow and the sack truck, a trio which, on the face of it, would probably be more at home resurfacing the M4 than making life easier in the garden.

The pickaxe has many obvious uses such as lifting stones or breaking heavy, compacted soil. But what about getting under obstinate tree roots, moving shrubs and digging holes for fence posts? If you garden on stony chalk you will need one to dig your bean trench too!

There's one type of wheelbarrow worthy of special mention, which is based on the builder's barrow design. They have a strong but light frame with comfortably spaced handles, ample capacity in a galvanised steel bin, a pneumatic tyre and a tipping bar. Wooden barrows may win in the aesthetics stakes but can be heavy enough to lift even when empty. As for plastic versions, they're fine if your garden waste is confined to vegetation but no good for the rough stuff.

IDEA 19, *To prune or not to prune*, talks you through the tools needed for pruning.

Try another idea...

A sack truck is another must. Why risk your back heaving around bags of compost, heavy stones, pots and containers, when you can slide a sack truck underneath and wheel it along like a doll's pram? Its versatility will amaze you.

Another rarely mentioned tool is a besom. Traditionally used for removing worm casts from manicured lawns, it's hard to beat when it comes to general sweeping. Make it yourself if you have access to a bundle of birch twigs and a hazel rod for the handle.

A good pair of secateurs is vital. Buy the best, look after them and you'll be well rewarded. But only use them for the job for which they were intended – which is cutting stems no more that 1cm thick. Anything bigger, and you'll just blunt them. Be patient, and fetch a small pruning saw or loppers instead.

'But remember there are no flowers without tools and no tools without a garage to keep them in.'
From *The Accidental Gardener's Almanac* by MICHAEL POWELL

Defining idea...

MAN AND MACHINES

If you are gardening acres of land, then machine tools have to be a priority. However, in most gardens they're an indulgent luxury and a one-off trip to the tool hire shop is more sensible.

But where needs must, invest in one top-of-the-range item that will last and actually get used – more about that in a moment.

Garden machinery tends to begrudge being disturbed, but in early spring it's time to drag your mowers and your strimmers coughing and spluttering out into the open.

As for that one serious investment, if you have large areas of grass, then the latest ride-on self-mulching mowers are heaven sent. Under normal mowing conditions – that's regularly mown, dry grass – there really is no sign of grass cuttings left lying around at all and, contrary to expectation, it produces less thatch than more conventional mowing methods. And because of the constant fine mulching, which acts as a feed, your grass will stay greener for longer.

A strimmer – petrol driven, electric or battery operated – will complement the magical mulcher above, getting into all those nooks and crannies. The battery model is the quietest and you can strim away happily for at least half an hour before recharging.

Clean your tools regularly but, come the end of the autumn, clean, oil and – where appropriate – sharpen them, because as all responsible gardeners know, garden tools are for life, not just for Christmas.

Q   What hand tools do I need to go with my fork and spade?

A   *Simply a hand fork, trowel and some shears. In practice you may need more than one trowel as they do seem to like hiding amongst the plants! When choosing shears make sure they have good buffers between the handles – less jarring for you.*

Q   Where does my hoe rank in the usefulness league?

A   *About half way down. A hoe is at home in the veg patch. (Hoeing flowerbeds has to be done more carefully, lest you behead a young plant.) Use the Dutch hoe to chop off weed seedlings, the draw hoe to make seed drills and earth up potatoes.*

How did it go?

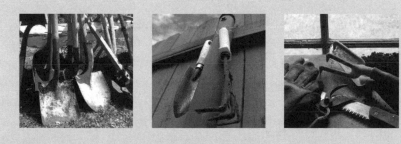

9

Grass roots

There's a moment in *Asterix in Britain* in which a gent is seen tending his immaculate lawn one blade at a time. 'Another two thousand years of loving care,' he says, 'and I think it'll make quite a decent bit of turf.'

We're obsessed with lawns. Perfect carpets of emerald green are the aristocrats of gardens, a symbol of horticultural class and the hallmark of stately homes the world over.

This obsession can sap your energy and take up precious time and money. But with a bit of seasonal savvy you can transform rough turf into something that at least resembles centre court at Wimbledon – albeit at the end of the fortnight, rather than the start.

The first step is to know when and how to cut your grass. Regular cutting helps to invigorate the growing tips so, for this reason, mowing the lawn should be seen as a year-round job – including winter, when just a couple of cuts can make all the difference come spring. There's more to master mowing than meets the eye. Cut it too short, and the grass won't retain enough water; too long, and it will bend over and stop new shoots from getting any sun. Consistency is the key. If you do let the

Here's an idea for you...

Try sowing wildflowers like field poppies (*Papaver rhoeas*), cornflowers (*Centaurea cyanus*) and Ox-eye daisies (*Chrysantheum leucanthemum*) where the grass has given up the ghost. Or you could plant a camomile lawn – a favourite for hundreds of years. It forms a dense mat of foliage, which releases a heady smell when trodden on. Non-flowering varieties are best.

lawn grow too long then don't cut it right back in one go, as this will cause scalping. As a general rule never remove more than one-third of the leaf in any single mowing.

Watering is as crucial as it is easy to overlook. Hose pipe bans permitting, don't leave it too late to give your lawn a good soaking as turf that's already turned yellow or brown is unlikely to be revived, and only new shoots that manage to grow through will save it.

Of course lawns are for living with, so if you share your lawn with children, let alone dogs, then you need to accept that it's going to take a battering. Give your grass a chance to bounce back by over-seeding it during autumn, when the seed has most chance to get established. Simply sprinkle small amounts of seed over the whole lawn to thicken up thin areas.

For larger, bald patches turfing may be more suitable, and is quicker but more expensive. But don't throw your money away by letting it dry out – just lay it! For reseeding, fork the whole area, re-level the soil, and sow at the full recommended rate. Easy!

As for grass type – seed or turf – the current vogue is for dwarf perennial rye, which offers all the traditional toughness of rye but the added attraction of ornamental leaves. It's a creeping variety of grass, which spreads underground before sending up new shoots. It's quick to establish, and quick to recover from damage, which is why it's favoured by the sports industry.

For a more delicate effect you may want to look into clump-forming grasses such as fescue or bent. It's true that their resistance to constant wear and tear, and to disease, is limited, but on the other hand you can cheer yourself up with a chuckle over their names.

For more ideas about how to make your garden child-friendly – and child resistant – see IDEA 29, *Danger – children at play.*

Try another idea...

DO WALK ON THE GRASS

It's also important to aerate an established lawn by forking it in both spring and autumn. This helps to alleviate compaction and helps drainage, but it can be an arduous task. Alternatives include mechanical aerators which you can hire, or specially spiked overshoes which do the job as you simply walk up and down. Drainage can be further improved by applying a top dressing of six parts sand to three parts soil and one part peat substitute. This can then be brushed into the holes.

Scarifying is also a crucial part of your new routine, and removes dead grass and moss. This allows air to reach the new shoots and gives them a chance to grow. Scarifying is the best treatment you can give a lawn and you can do it at anytime of year (except the depths of winter) by using a spring-tined rake. It will also give you a workout as satisfying and intense as anything you'll get in the gym!

Spring is the best time to feed your lawn and, whether you choose a quick- or slow-release product, don't stint on quality and always check the label for any risk to children or pets.

'Until man duplicates a blade of grass, nature can laugh at his so-called scientific knowledge.'
THOMAS EDISON

Defining idea...

So, just to recap – keep cutting all year, scarify when you fancy it, feed and weed in spring, and get to grips with those bare patches in the autumn.

Q We've got kids and we want them to enjoy the garden but their toys aren't really compatible with a lush lawn. Any tips?

A Leaving a paddling pool or sand pit in the same spot for as little as two days can kill everything underneath it. It's also a good idea to move swings and slides on a regular basis – or you can designate an area that you are prepared to let suffer, and then deal with it later.

Q Other than flagstones and decking, what are the alternatives to grass?

A Whisper it, but artificial grass is becoming popular. It's made from polypropylene, and is available in a choice of colours. But while it may save on the mowing, it's pretty unforgiving when it comes to small elbows and knees.

Q Where's the best place to buy seed?

A Avoid paying for seed that comes ready packaged with pretty pictures of a perfect lawn. Far cheaper to buy in bulk from a nursery that supplies it not only loose, but for different types of conditions too.

10

Support network

Do your delphiniums droop as soon as you look at them? Your lupins lean at the first breath of wind? Then you need support.

We all have our down days, lackadaisical days, when everything seems too much trouble. Plants are no different. Turn your back for a minute and they can come over all floppy and limp as they search for something to lean on. And that's where the keen-eyed gardener comes in, armed with a range of natural and man-made structures and gizmos that will give trees and plants a bit of backbone.

BOLSTERING THE BORDER

If your border is to keep its looks throughout the summer, herbaceous plants need staking. This needs to be done in April or May when the plants are still young and stout, and also to give the plants' lush new growth the chance to smother their crutches.

Here's an idea for you...

If you've got enough space, think about cultivating your own clump of hazel. It's a fast grower, produces long straight rods, and its early spring catkins are an added bonus. If cut around March, when the sap is rising, it's extremely pliable and can be put to endless uses in the garden.
It's particularly good for sweet pea tripods, and used together with thin, flexible pieces of willow (whips) woven through the uprights, you have a natural frame, just made for the creeping, curling tendrils of the sweet pea.

Tall plants with heavy flowers such as delphiniums, sunflowers, and hollyhocks, need individual supports – usually bamboo canes. Tie them in when the plant is 10–15cm high, supporting it loosely with garden string. Keep doing this as the plant grows until it's about waist high, and then by the time it flowers the plant will be tall enough to hide the cane.

But remember to put something over the top of the cane, such as an old yoghurt pot or cork, otherwise you run the risk of resembling your black-eyed Suzy.

Other strong performers like monkshood (*Aconitum*), daisies, peonies and dahlias, benefit from the all-round support of metal hoops, link stakes or a personal favourite, pea sticks.

The real beauty of pea sticks is that they look natural because they allow the plants to grow through them, and cut out the need for any string or ties. Felled or fallen trees and forest trimmings are a great source, but failing that your own garden prunings will do. Choose twiggy bits with a strong central stem, and cut at an angle to make them easier to push into the ground. They last for years, so you can keep a selection of different heights for different-sized plants.

Look at a mature tree, with its stout trunk and majestic spread, and it's hard to imagine it ever needed any kind of support. But in its first few years hugging and kind words will have been no substitute for a good staking. This will have helped it survive high winds and blustering storms while its stabilising roots took hold.

IDEA 5, *Indian summer*, features other 'things to do' to keep the border looking good.

Try another idea...

How to go about staking a tree, however, is the subject of some horticultural debate. Should the stake be straight or slanted into the prevailing wind? Should it be short, to make the tree do some of the work itself, or tall, to give maximum support? It's worth experimenting to find the method that works best for your situation but there is one key rule that all arboriculturists agree on – stake as you plant, sinking the post (a strong one that will last for a couple years) into the planting hole before the tree. Do it the other way round, and you risk driving it through precious roots.

A tree is a big investment, so two more things to remember. Tie the tree to the stake with a special tree tie – one with a spacer between the tree and the buckle – and place the buckle against the stake, not the tree, to stop chafing. And don't forget to check the supports at least twice a year, loosening them when necessary.

FRUIT AND VEG PROPS

Most veg grows happily without support but runner beans and peas must have a framework.

Defining idea...

'*Go 'n get some more sticks,*' ordered Selina, '*... Look here, in the kitchen garden, there's a pile of old pea sticks. Fetch as many as you can carry, and then go back and bring some more!*'

'*But I say,*' began Harold, amazedly, scarce knowing his sister, and with a vision of a frenzied gardener, pea stickless and threatening retribution.

'*Go and fetch 'em quick!*' shouted Selina, stamping with impatience.
From *Dream Days*, by KENNETH GRAHAM

43

Beans need canes or hazel stems, and peas, strangely enough, need pea sticks. If neither are available a nylon, wide-mesh net can be strung between supports 2m tall for beans, and 1.5m for peas.

Runner bean frames, whether arranged in wigwams or rows with cross support at the top, should be firmly tied and well grounded. Given the right amount of compost and water, these climbers put on tremendous growth and provide a ready-made sail for any strong winds gusting through.

Raspberry canes need help staying upright and in line – two characteristics which make them much easier to pick. They need a strong frame of end poles 180cm high with cross wires spaced at heights of 50, 100 and 150cms. Place cross slats at the top to take the net and you won't have to share your fruit with the birds.

How did it go?

Q   Do I need to support my fruit trees, or can I let them get on with it?

A   *Free-standing trees can be left unsupported once they're established but you should keep an eye out for a particularly heavy crop. There is nothing more frustrating than a bough full of fruit breaking under the strain. A cracked branch can be propped up to allow the fruit to ripen but it will have to be severed cleanly at the end of the season.*

Q   Can you use plants to support other plants for a more natural look?

A   *Yes, this works particularly well with climbers. A rambling rose or* Clematis montana *wandering up and through a mature tree (perhaps one with little summer interest) can look spectacular.*

11

Gnome-free zone

Not all garden ornaments need have pointed hats and fishing rods, especially if you take the time to design and make your own.

Sir Charles Ischam has a lot to answer for. Not for this Victorian a great scientific discovery, a great invention, or even a great expedition. No, this 'eccentric spiritualist' as he is often called, was the man responsible for introducing the garden gnome to Britain in 1847.

Over 150 years later and while the imps are still popular, there are plenty of more ingenious ways to bring a touch of mystery to your borders. Here we look at how to acquire a work of art for nothing – your own Hepworth or Epstein. But don't reach for the chisel just yet, as it's your powers of observation and improvisation that matter.

Here's an idea for you... **Inspired? Well, fashioning a garden seat from a branch of fallen willow will take all of ten minutes to make. A 2m length sits on two shorter pieces, with the supports cut with a slight hollow to house the seat. It's neither nailed nor glued. The weight of the seat is sufficient to hold it securely.**

SET IN STONE

There are many types and shapes of stone from shards of flint to massive sandstone boulders called sarsens. And while it's unlikely prehistoric man built Stonehenge or the Avebury Circle with gardens in mind, he was heading in the right direction.So where do you source your raw materials? Building sites, where old barns, mills or cottages are being restored or converted, are havens for smaller pieces of sarsen. Farmers churn up a good number each year too and would welcome a willing pair of hands to help move a few.

Flint is another great resource and again any farmer will cheer you on as you rid him of the cause of many a blunted ploughshare. Flint comes in all sizes and colours, from white through to beige, burnt orange to black. As a result, its decorative uses are endless. The bird bath, on the previous page, was made some fifteen years ago from flint. A piece of old piping was used as a mould to make the stem, and a round plastic basin for the bath itself. By removing the moulds before they are totally set, you can wash off some mortar with a fierce hose to expose the flint.

SYLVAN BAZAAR

Of course, the key to this rural foraging is to ask first. Dismantling a dry stone wall, or taking other pieces of natural stone that obviously serve a practical purpose, is not only illegal but stupid.

A few years ago, one of us discovered a large stone that turned out to be an old gatepost, half buried next to the wooden post that had replaced it. The farmer was only too glad to root it out with a digger and place it under a French window, where it has become a formidable seat. And not only was it free, but it's also sustainable, eye-catching and will no doubt outlast anything that could have been bought from the local DIY superstore.

Being much lighter than stone, wood is often more easily available. Who can honestly say they haven't been taken by a smoothed piece of driftwood washed up on the tide line, or a gnarled bough, recently crashed to earth? Garden designers love them and import them from far and wide – which rather negates their recycled value, but that's another story. They can be seen dried, cleaned, even polished and for sale at mortgage-threatening prices.

But you don't have to reach for the cheque book, and even beachcombing isn't necessary, particularly if you live some way from the coast. Forest floors, particularly in autumn and better still after a storm, are a virtual sylvan bazaar. Use recently fallen material only. Dead or rotten wood should be left well alone to provide a haven for insects, especially stag beetles.

The hornbeam log shown overleaf was discovered in the Belgian Ardennes that was brought back in the boot of the car. The ends have been sawn parallel and it's been cleaned and polished. That's all. It's a wonderfully tactile piece and has a human's muscular form. In the summer it's used as a garden table, in winter it is taken indoors and looks perfectly at home. Eat your heart out Henry Moore.

There are more joinery skills to be had in IDEA 40, _Structurally sound_, while in IDEA 46, _Up the garden path_, patios and paths are laid to rest.

Try another idea...

'**We demand that garden gnomes are no longer ridiculed and that they be released into their natural habitat.**'
Statement by the Garden Gnome Liberation Front

Defining idea...

How did it go?

Q   **I've tried making my own bird bath but just mention the word water and it starts to leak. Any tips?**

A   *Skim mortar over the inside of bath, allow this to dry thoroughly and then paint with at least two coats of yacht varnish.*

Q   **So you don't like gnomes?**

A   *No, not particularly. But that's not to say that some stylised ornaments, such as animals, aren't attractive, if not more so than a perfect replica of an animal. The photo below right shows stones with black metal painted heads and legs (an idea of Dutch artist Cees van Swieten). The stones were selected for size only and at first didn't appear especially appropriate as sheep. Add the head and legs, however, and the whole flock was brought to life.*

12

Slugging it out

There's more than one way to defeat gardener's number-one foe.

Slugs and snails, like weeds and aphids, are something that gardeners have to learn to live with. Even those who declare chemical warfare on the critters will soon discover that it takes more than a few pellets of metaldehyde (the active ingredient in most slug pellets) to defeat these malevolent molluscs.

But that isn't to suggest you should simply throw in the trowel and accept that your hostas will be shredded and your delphiniums decimated.

Your garden is likely to be home to several kinds of slugs and snails, but it's the grey field slug that does most damage, closely followed by the chestnut and garden slugs. And while the large black ones may be the easiest to pick off, they probably do less damage than the other three.

Snails are said to be less destructive, particularly the banded ones, although large, grey common garden snails, and smaller strawberry snails, with their flattened shell, have voracious appetites.

Every gardener has a favourite way of ridding the beds of slugs and snails, from best bitter to copper tape, but we would like to take this opportunity to denounce barrier methods once and for all! We've tried the lot, from broken egg shells to grit, gravel to ash, even used coffee grounds. But it's not long before the buggers have decided that a dish of young lupin shoots is well worth a little discomfort.

Copper tape is more effective but, as with copper-impregnated slug mats, is only suitable for pots and containers.

KEEPING THE BALANCE

Officially the jury is still out on whether slug pellets really do harm wildlife by killing off the thrushes and frogs that eat the poisonous cadavers. But until there's concrete evidence to the contrary, surely it makes sense to use a more wildlife-friendly aluminium sulphate-based pellet instead. Also effective are beer traps, sunk into the ground and filled with

Here's an idea for you...

With delphiniums choose good strong plants in the first place and grow them on in pots, where it's easier to deter the enemy. Cutting back the main growing shoot will allow the plant to grow more shoots and gather its strength. Plant out when it's about 25cm high and it should be robust enough to fight off an attack.

For extra peace of mind, remove the top and the bottom of a plastic bottle and then place over the plant. Smear a layer of petroleum jelly round the rim for a bit of extra protection. If you can get your delphiniums through one year, they're likely to be strong enough to win the fight in future years.

your least favourite brew. Half a grapefruit does just as well but these devices are indiscriminate and will take out ground beetles too, an important slug predator.

IDEA 35, *Wildlife friendly,* **goes into more detail about how to attract wildlife to your garden.**

Try another idea...

Other tips include keeping your garden free of leaf litter and plant debris, which gives the slugs somewhere to chill out during the day. Others, however, argue that weeds, especially dandelions, can entice slugs away from your blooms, while one prize-winning hosta grower claims to plant 'sacrificial hosta seedlings' as a way of saving his best specimens.

The best form of defence is, of course, attack and although pricey, nematodes certainly work. These naturally occurring parasites eat the slugs and you can boost the numbers in the soil by mixing a packet of the microscopic bugs with water and applying as per the instructions. You'll soon notice a lot less devastation in your borders.

But by far the best way to beat the molluscs is to hunt them down yourself at night. Yes, the neighbours' curtains may twitch as you crawl around, torch in hand, but as well as fostering a much closer affinity with your plants, catching the little bleeders at work is extremely rewarding.

Once caught, how to dispatch them is up to you. Under foot, in a bucket of salty water or for the truly beneficent, bagged up for later release into the countryside.

'Slug-resistant plants are a myth.'
PAULINE PEARS, Henry Doubleday Research Association

Defining idea...

But be aware that nature maintains a certain number of snails in any one garden, so clearing them away is a bit like painting the Forth Bridge, and there's always a clutch of baby monsters waiting to take their place at the table.

LET THE WILDLIFE WORK FOR YOU

The trouble with all these remedies is that you need to mount a continuous campaign, renewing the treatment after rain, or setting the alarm clock for the middle of the night to search out the offenders. For a longer-term approach, try encouraging some allies into the garden.

A pond will enhance the frog population, while a pellet-free garden is more likely to attract nesting birds. And if you don't feed birds after June, they'll be more likely to seek out the pests in your garden instead.

A cool, damp place, such as the bottom of a stone wall or behind a water butt will encourage toads to set up residence, and if you live near water, then encourage ducks and moorhens into the garden – both thrive on slugs.

How did it go?

Q Any more suggestions about what to do with my hostas, which are still taking a battering?

A *The best solution is to choose the right type of hosta. The family* Hosta sieboldiana *is the one to grow. Its large, spectacular leaves are on the whole too tough for slugs and snails. If an adventurous creature does have a go one bite seems enough.*

Q Any plants that slugs and snails don't seem to like much?

A *Foxgloves, euphorbia, astilbe and sweet peas seem to be pretty low down the pecking order.*

13

Growing under glass

Whether you're pottering in a top-of-the-range greenhouse or hunched over a cold frame, growing under glass can deliver miraculous results.

With the light, warmth and shelter provided by glass, for once the foibles of the British weather need not concern you. Exotic flowers, tender vegetables, cuttings and seeds can all get a head start but bear in mind that gardening in a greenhouse is a labour-intensive affair, although if the Victorian glasshouse gardener could produce a pineapple for the Christmas table, anything's possible!

You first need to ask yourself what you're interested in growing and how much time you can set aside to grow it. If you're working full-time or have a young family, investing in a free-standing greenhouse with all its accessories and accoutrements could leave you fraught and frustrated, and with no time to do your investment justice.

Here's an idea for you...

If you don't have space in your garden for a greenhouse then buy a cloche. This is a portable frame covered with glass or plastic which can bring temporary shelter to delicate plants and early flowers. Large cloches or mini tunnels can also be used to warm small areas of soil prior to spring vegetable planting.

Instead think about a cold frame or mini lean-to greenhouses, which are cheaper and much less demanding. These can still give plants like fuchsias, pelargoniums (the large-flowered geraniums grown outdoors in the summer), dahlias and trendy cannas the winter protection they need, as well as providing you with the space to start preparing the blooms for next year's pots and borders.

A GARDENER'S COMMAND CENTRE

But if you have got the time and the inclination to get stuck into some serious propagating, then treat yourself to a free-standing greenhouse. But before you dig deep, however, you need to decide whether you're going for an aluminium or wooden frame.

Aluminium is light and less expensive, while a wooden one (usually red cedar) is more costly but will give you the option of having wooden sides a metre high all round, providing insulation on very cold and very hot days. You might also want to consider leaving one full side as glass to allow more light in during the summer for tender vegetables and fruit. But whatever you decide, go for one as big as possible, as there's no such thing as a greenhouse that's too big. (And remember to site it running east to west if possible.)

Aluminium greenhouses usually come in a pack for 'easy' self-assembly, but will need to be erected on firm ground or concrete slabs. A wooden greenhouse is trickier and will need footings (concrete underpinning) and a course of bricks, which needs to be dead square because the panes of glass have been cut to fit and don't bend easily! At this stage it's worth setting a pipe or piece of hose through the footings too, so that the electrics can be threaded through later.

With average DIY skills this is a project worth attempting – after all, all gardeners need a project and what better one than this. But if the intricacies of plumb lines and stretcher bonds are beyond you, then best call in the professionals.

To see what's involved in propagation and to help you decide on the type and size of greenhouse that suits, see IDEA 4, Don't pay the nurseryman.

Try another idea...

LIFE ON THE INSIDE

Even if you aren't growing directly into the soil, it's still a good idea to have soil beds along either side of your greenhouse. They help the humidity and allow you to 'dampen down' when things get too dry and hot. But you'll need to change the soil every couple of years.

And toasty as your greenhouse may sometimes feel, without a little help a greenhouse is not 'frost free'. A lean-to has the added advantage of the warmth from a house wall, but an unheated greenhouse is only a degree or two warmer than outside. Basic protection for overwintering plants can be provided by bubble wrap, pinned or clipped on the inside of the glass.

As with any hobby, gadgets and gizmos are vital, and one accessory no self-respecting greenhouse should be seen without is a self-opening vent. These miraculous contraptions work of their own accord, keep an eye on the temperature for you, and open or close mysteriously when things get too hot or cold.

'After working in a greenhouse for a year I grew nine inches.'
Noted by ALAN TITCHMARSH in *Trowel and Error.*

Defining idea...

Staging and shelving are also a must and can be bought as a kit or homemade. Then, in order of importance, come a radio (well, you don't want to become totally isolated from the outside world!), propagators, heating and a watering system. Heating will not only keep you warm but a minimum night-time temp of 4–5°C will be sufficient to satisfy the needs of a wide range of plants. And, on sunny days, shading may be necessary. While blinds are widely available, special shade paint, applied to the glass and then washed off in the autumn, is a much cheaper option.

How did it go?

Q   Greenhouses seem expensive and complicated to put up. As my garden is out of sight of any neighbours I was thinking about a polytunnel, is this a good substitute?

A   *A polytunnel is a good alternative and much used by commercial growers. However, plastic doesn't let in as much light as glass, especially as it ages. Also remember to secure the tunnel well against the winds and make the frame tall enough to work in it with comfort.*

Q   How important is it to clean the greenhouse – can I leave it to the rain?

A   *A clean greenhouse lets in more light and keeps disease to a minimum so it's a good idea. Give the glass a thorough clean in October/November, washing off any shade paint applied in the summer. Give the inside a good clean once all the spring plants are safely bedded out; wash and sterilise all pots, trays and propagators before use.*

14

Your own little powerhouse part I

Bulbs and corms are just packed with energy. Treat 'em right and you can enjoy years of colour.

From hyacinths to tulips, crocuses to snowdrops, bulbs are one of the safest bets when it comes to guaranteed spring colour. There are also more varieties than you can shake a stick at, but whether you're a devotee of daffs or addicted to alliums, there are a few general rules to follow.

YOU PAYS YOUR MONEY...

It pays to buy your bulbs early as the condition in which they're stored is just as important as the soil you eventually plant them in. They need to have been kept cool and dry, not hot and bothered on a shop shelf.

Here's an idea for you...

Planting crocuses in the grass works especially well. Try mixing mauve and purple *C. tomasinianus*. But make sure you choose an area of lawn that you're happy to leave unmown until all the foliage dies back. This will encourage them to carrying on flowering each year.

You also need to avoid the temptation of buying a job lot. Of course, they look good value but with bulbs the biggest really are the best, as they tend to be the ones that produce the best blooms on the strongest stems. The other bonus about buying them loose is that you can check each one, making sure they're not soft or diseased.

The difference between bulbs and corms, by the way, is that bulbs, like an onion, are a mass of fleshy, food-storing leaves, enclosing a bud. A corm, such as a crocus, is a swollen stem that usually only lasts one season, to be replaced by another underground.

COLD STORAGE

Bulbs need the winter's cold to get them going in spring which is why there's always such a rush of activity in the autumn, as gardeners are faced with a heap of the scaly brutes to intern.

With daffs and crocuses, get them planted early, before the end of September if possible, as they're already set to send out their roots. Leave tulips until November, and most of the others can be fitted in somewhere between, spreading the load on your back and knees at the same time.

Plant them at roughly three times their own depth, unless otherwise specified. That's about 25–30cm for your average daff or tulip, while smaller ones, such as chionodoxa and scilla, should go in a hole roughly 10cm deep. As for spacing, with all bulbs it's a good idea to plant them in clumps, and while theoretically you should leave up to 15cm between the bigger bulbs, let's face it, when you've got a few hundred to plant, who's measuring?

Bulbs enjoy free-draining soil, so if you garden on clay add some grit to the planting hole, and the more random your planting, the better the overall effect. Drop a handful of bulbs on the ground and plant them where they land.

Certain bulbs, notably the snowdrop (*Galanthus*), snowflake (*Leucojum*) and winter aconite (*Eranthis*) need to be planted 'in the green', which means just after flowering, with the leaves still intact. (You should be able to buy them like this from the garden centre.) Make sure they don't dry out.

Once in the ground, bulbs need little maintenance but will appreciate a handful of bonemeal after flowering to store up energy for next year.

LEAVE THE LEAVES

Once they've done their bit, resist the urge to cut back the dying leaves too soon, as you'll weaken the bulb and reduce its flowering potential for next year. Yes, deadhead them, but only cut down the foliage once it starts to yellow.

Tubers and rhizomes may sound like a medical conditions, but there's more colour to be had from these crusty little customers in IDEA 39, *Your own little powerhouse part II*.

Try another idea...

'Bulbs are cheap, so we should refuse to feel guilty about splashing around quantities of them in our mixed borders. Most can stay where they are planted for years, either increasing or gradually petering out. That said, I have to admit to spending more on bulbs, annually, than on any other kind of plant.'
CHRISTOPHER LLOYD

Defining idea...

59

If you choose to leave your bulbs in situ all year (which seems to us the eminently more sensible option!), it pays to dig them up and separate them every few years to prevent overcrowding. And if you've got any particularly expensive varieties in the ground, such as one of the giant alliums, mark their position so you don't inadvertently disturb them when they're dormant.

Daffs look their best naturalized in grass but if planting in the spring border choose dwarf narcissi as a good way of avoiding the perennial problem of daffodils with withered foliage. Varieties such as N. *cyclamineus* and N. *pseudonarcissus* (Lent Lily) have much smaller leaves that are easily concealed by other plants. Complement them with a blanket of blue grape hyacinth (*Muscari*).

Alliums are true show stoppers, particularly the giant varieties such as A. *giganteum*, with its fabulous 12cm spherical heads. There are hundreds of other varieties of this common onion genus, from the small, yellow-flowered A. *moly* (golden garlic) to the medium size A. *cristophi*, with its metallic pink flowers.

Tulips are in a class of their own – not so good in subsequent years but fabulous in year one, so you should treat yourself to fresh bulbs annually. Planted in November, in bold groups or containers, their form and intensity of colour can't be beaten. There's a shade and shape to suit every taste, from the frilly pink parrot tulip 'Fantasy' to the lily flowered 'Red Shine', and the almost black Darwin variety 'Queen of the Night'. Flowering from March to May, they really do match their pictures in the catalogues!

There are hundreds of summer, autumn and winter flowering bulbs too, as well as those that have been bred specially for fragrance, foliage or floristry.

Q Why do so few of my bulbs ever flower?

A *Chances are they're overcrowded and starved unless they have been eaten by mice! They (bulbs not mice) don't mind being close together as long as they've got plenty of light and you give them some feed as soon as the leaves show. What they hate is dry dark spots under trees or a dense hedge. Bulb blindness is easily cured by lifting and replanting in well-fertilised soil.*

Q Any suggestions for bulbs that work well underneath a tree?

A *The hardy cyclamen is great for naturalizing underneath trees. You'll be amazed by the ability of the delicate pink flowers and marbled foliage to push through the ground in autumn (*C. neapolitanum*) or December to March (*C. coum*).*

How did it go?

15

Small but perfectly formed

You don't have to own a plot the size of a football pitch to make vegetable gardening worthwhile.

The crunch of a home-grown runner bean, the sweetness of a pod-fresh pea, the sheer productivity of a simple potato. This is how the vegetable gardener measures success.

Growing vegetables is all about getting back to basics: the sowing, the nurturing, the eating. It doesn't matter what you grow or where you grow it. You can devote a whole plot to curly kale if that's what takes your fancy. And you really don't have to grow broccoli if you don't like it.

ROTATION, ROTATION, ROTATION

But it's not all anarchy down on the allotment and there are some simple rules to follow. Think about how labour-intensive your crops are going to be for a starter; are they an add-on to the other, more pleasurable, pursuits in the garden, or your *raison d'être* for pulling on your wellies in the first place?

Here's an idea for you... **Growing veg from seed is time consuming, so why not buy some young vegetable plants at the same time as you buy your summer bedding. Go for healthy, stocky plants but don't buy until the frosts have passed, unless you've a greenhouse to protect them.**

Will you be able to freeze your veg at the end of the day? While it's tempting to cram in as much as possible, have you thought what you're going to do with armfuls of runner beans and sackloads of potatoes come harvest time (friends and relatives can only take so much, you know)?

Then there's crop rotation – sounds serious but it's a proven way of maximising production and minimising pests and diseases.

Vegetables fall into three basic groups and the idea is that you move these groups around your patch each year.

- Brassicas include cabbages, broccoli, sprouts and cauliflower (the latter notoriously difficult to grow). They all prefer alkaline soil, so you'll need to add some lime if yours is on the acid side. This should also help prevent club root.
- A second group – the roots – includes carrots, parsnips, beetroot and potatoes, and needs a balanced, high-potash fertiliser (no manure) adding to the soil a few days before sowing. Carrot fly are attracted to the smell of carrot leaves (especially when crushed) as well as recently dug soil, so try to introduce some scented, ornamental plants nearby to keep the pests at bay, and keep the soil around your carrots firmed down.
- All the other veg, from legumes (beans and peas), to leeks, spinach, corn, courgettes and onions, fall into a third category, and all respond well to plenty of manure or compost, dug into the ground in autumn or winter.

If you decide to grow a selection from one group only, say runner beans, leeks, courgettes and spinach, then you don't need to worry about rotation. Just keep adding loads of muck. Plant lettuces around the edge of the well-manured

You can get better acquainted with the concept of companion planting in IDEA 32, *Alright mate*.

Try another idea...

bits, and water all the vegetables regularly, especially when getting them started.

Broad beans are toughies, so sow these outside in the autumn. Other beans and courgettes can be sown straight into the ground (once it has warmed up) but they'll get off to a quicker start if sown in pots under glass, in early spring. Sow leeks in a metre-long piece of plastic guttering. Once they've germinated, slide the whole lot off into the veg patch to grow on until big enough to handle. Plant out by sinking each seedling into a 25cm hole, made by a dibber or trowel handle. (You may want to trim the roots and tops a little to make this easier.) Fill each hole with water to secure the seedling in place.

Spinach and all root crops don't like being moved, so sew these directly into their final growing positions.

EYES BIGGER THAN YOUR STOMACH?

Don't try to fit too much in, and remember to leave enough room to work. If your soil is easily waterlogged, build in some paths or raised beds, so there's no excuse for not working in wet weather. Vegetables that grow upwards are useful in a small patch, runner beans especially. But do start picking them when they're young and slim, and not when they've become thick and coarse.

'A cauliflower is a cabbage with a college education.'
MARK TWAIN

Defining idea...

65

Defining idea...

'To get the best results, you must talk to your vegetables.'
PRINCE CHARLES

You can also grow veg that you just keep picking, such as perpetual spinach (fantastically healthy and it will re-grow easily if kept well watered) and cut-and-come-again lettuce.

If you haven't got room for a vegetable patch, don't dismiss the humble tub or container. Although this is small-scale veg growing, it's still a viable alternative. Potatoes in pots work particularly well, and one chitted seed potato in a 25-litre pot should produce 45 plus new spuds.

You could also try tomatoes, aubergines or peppers, courgettes, lettuce, onions, carrot or peas. Use plastic containers or line terracotta ones with plastic to keep from drying out. If possible, set up a watering system – a hose with outlets to each container – that will trickle water easily to each pot.

Letting vegetables loose throughout the garden is another way of overcoming space restrictions. Their lush green leaves, brightly coloured flowers and stalks certainly don't look out of place. Grow runner beans on an arch, edge beds with coloured varieties of lettuce, or add drama to the back of the border with globe artichokes. But try and remember what's been where, so you can move your veg around from year to year.

Q   With the right soil conditions and frequent watering, can anyone grow monster veg for the show table?

How did it go?

A   *Growing vegetables for show takes years of practice and bucket loads of experience (and manure). However, there's nothing to stop you having a go in your local garden club's annual show. All you need are a few straight runner beans or a group of courgettes or carrots the same size. If all else fails you can always enter the 'most unusually shaped vegetable' class!*

Q   The 'other half' insists the garden's for flowers not veg. How do I go about renting an allotment?

A   *Sadly nearly half the allotments in Britain were sold off to developers in the 1970s and 1980s. As a result, though, you'll probably have to join a waiting list. Contact your local council or wander along to an allotment and have a chat with the tenants.*

16

Living with the enemy

Some gardeners are obsessed with their destruction; others see them as an extra splash of colour. But whatever you think of weeds, you can't ignore them.

If you're happy to spray and blast chemicals around your garden, indiscriminately killing anything that gets in the way, then this chapter's not for you. If, on the other hand, you're prepared to take on the likes of the pernicious bindweed and the dastardly dandelion without threatening the existence of everything else that lives in the garden, then read on.

Many weeds are of course wild flowers that would be greeted with whoops of joy if spotted swaying on the edge of a cornfield, or growing amidst the hawthorn and the elder of a hedgerow.

Here's an idea for you...

Some weeds even have their uses. Horsetail is rich in silica, for instance, so a few handfuls crushed up and added to the watering can will give plants a good protective coating, making them much harder for insects to chew.
Cover a bundle of nettles in 10 litres of water and leave for a few weeks. Then strain off the liquid, add it to water in a ratio of 1:5, and you have an excellent liquid feed.

They are incredibly successful plants, usually natives that have had centuries to adapt to the environment in which they grow, making them extremely hardy and able to reproduce quickly and easily.

This makes them a tricky and devious enemy. But on the upside, thriving weeds are a sure sign that you have good, rich soil.

The best course of action when tackling weeds is some form of coexistence. Let nature take complete control and it won't be long before the whole garden is strangled by the most pernicious weeds. But become obsessed with uprooting them, and you'll be left with precious little time to do anything else.

Defining idea...

'There is simply too much that we do not know to carelessly chuck noxious chemicals at a superficial problem like weeds.'
MONTY DON

The other benefit of this leniency is that some wildlife thrives on weeds. Without stinging nettles, for instance, peacock, small tortoiseshell and red admiral butterflies would have nowhere to lay their eggs. Isn't that reason alone to leave a few growing away unobtrusively at the back of the border?

KNOWING THE ENEMY

There are two main types of weed, the annual and the perennial.

Annuals like groundsel and cleavers (also called goose grass and like caviar to geese!) can generally be cleared by decapitating them with a hoe. This is best done on a dry day, when you can leave them to wither away. When the soil's damp, just pull them out by hand, a very therapeutic way to get closer to your plants.

Perennials, like stinging nettles, docks and dandelions, require a bit more effort and need digging out with a fork, root 'n all. Try to pull up the entire root or they can grow back from the merest piece left in the ground.

Ground elder can quite happily smother several square feet a year, while the horsetail does a lot of its work underground, entangling its black roots with those of other plants, making it even harder to get rid of. Thorough and repeated digging is the best approach, although it can have even the most dedicated organic gardener dreaming of weedkiller.

With its white trumpet flowers, there are certainly uglier plants than greater bindweed, which is actually part of the convolvulus family, cultivars of which we quite happily grow in the garden. The trouble is it doesn't know when to stop and will just keep on climbing unless kept in check. Organically, this means getting to grips with the fleshy, underground stems in early spring.

In case you haven't had enough of garden nasties take a look at IDEA 47, *Common diseases*, which lists all of them in gruesome detail.

Try another idea...

'A weed is a plant that is not only in the wrong place, but intends to stay.'
SARAH STEIN

Defining idea...

Defining
idea...

'Weeds are flowers too, once you get to know them.'
EEYORE in *Winnie the Pooh*

Perhaps the most invasive weed is Japanese knotweed, which has even been known to push up its shoots through thick concrete. Trying to defeat it is useless. You need to work round it, and just keep cutting it back.

UNDERCOVER OPERATIONS

In the absence of any organic weedkillers, mulching is also a good way of keeping the likes of bindweed and couch grass at bay. Remove what you can first of all and then spread a liberal layer of garden compost. This will starve the seeds of the light they need.

Other good mulches include grass clippings and straw, and although semi-permeable membranes look far from natural when exposed they do work, and fulfil the key role of letting in water but keeping out light.

Another way to keep weeds down is by planting plenty of ground cover plants. You need to do a thorough weeding job first, and keep going while the plants themselves get established, but the likes of *Heuchera*, creeping jenny (*Lysimachia nummularia*), hardy geranium, dead nettle (*Lamium*) and *Polygonum affine* – the friendly low-growing knotweed – should rise to the challenge.

Flame guns, or a hot-air paint stripper, are other ways to kill weeds that have sprung up in cracks and crevices on paths and patios. But beware of torching other plants nearby. To be honest, like leaf blowers and patio heaters, we don't really think they belong in the garden. Get down on your knees and do some proper weeding instead. It's good for the soul.

Q   **I've done as you said and now I've got a pile of dead and dying weeds. Should I put them on the compost heap?**

How did it go?

A   *Couch grass is a definite no-no, along with bindweed and horsetail. As for the others, it depends on your heap. If it's a hot one, which is often encouraged by adding in layers of grass cuttings, then the heat should be enough to kill any annual weed seeds. But if in doubt put them on the bonfire.*

Q   **I've got a few packets of old weed killer left over in the potting shed. Surely it wouldn't hurt to just use these up and then go organic?**

A   *Use them and you could burn a hole in your pocket as well as your garden's ecosystem. Many pesticides were recently banned and you could be fined for using them. Contact your local council to find out how to dispose of them safely.*

17

Oranges are not the only fruit

Picking fruit from your own tree is one of the ultimate horticultural highs. But before you can enjoy the sweet taste of success, you need to digest the bread and butter of growing fruit.

In the last thirty years, half of Britain's pear orchards and over 60% of its apple orchards have been destroyed. So what better time to start planting some of the fabulously named traditional varieties of British fruit, from the Kentish Fillbasket apple to the Vicar of Winkfield pear?

GOING PEAR-SHAPED

First up, always buy trees from a reputable supplier, who specialises in fruit and can answer the following questions.

Is the tree on the right rootstock? All fruit trees are grafted onto roots that have been specially selected for the size and shape of tree they will ultimately support. They are identified by the letter M followed by a number. The rootstock determines the vigour, resistance to pests and disease, and the eventual formation of the tree. Only buy trees on recommended rootstocks, as these are also the only ones guaranteed to be virus free.

- With apples, the stock ranges from M.27 for a small tree up to a couple of metres high, to the vigorous MM.111 that grows to 5m plus.
- Although there's no fully dwarfing rootstock for pears, Quince C is semi-dwarfing, and Quince A semi-vigorous.
- The rootstock for plums is St Julien A, a semi-dwarfing variety, which will pollinate with all other plums, damsons, gages, peaches, nectarines and apricots!

Here's an idea for you...

If you're really short of space but want a few different varieties in your garden, then try a 'family tree'. Two or three pears or apples can be grafted onto one rootstock giving different varieties from the one tree.

The second key question is: *How does the tree pollinate?* If the tree is a self-pollinator it will produce fruit all by itself. If not, it will need another tree, of a different variety, with which to 'mate'. Find out from a specialist book or nursery which varieties are compatible. It may be that one exists nearby in a neighbour's garden. If not, you'll need to do some matchmaking.

All apples need a compatible cross-pollinator, and while *Conference* and *William* pears are self-pollinators, they'll do better if paired off (ouch!). The cherry *Stella* and most plums are self-fertile, although planting two varieties of plum will improve the yield.

Finally, ask about growing conditions. Take account of the area you live in, the space and shelter you can offer the tree, and the soil type.

When planning where to put your fruit trees check out IDEA 15, *Small but perfectly formed*, to see how they will fit in with your veg patch.

Try another idea...

Apples are the least fussy and the hardiest of fruit. When planting, dig in plenty of manure and mulch, and feed in spring. There are hundreds of varieties to choose from, all of which will be different in some way whether it's in their taste, their resistance to diseases, or the time of year when they fruit. Some will even keep better than others.

Pears are for your heirs, as they say, and will take a few years before they start producing. They come early into blossom and late into fruit, so make sure they're not in a frost pocket, or be prepared to rush out with some fleece or net curtains if frost is forecast. They're not too fussy about soil but don't like shallow chalk and also enjoy a feed in spring.

Plums, liking rich moist ground, also blossom early and need a protected site. In heavy cropping years you may need to prop up their branches.

And don't forget the damsons! A neglected star of the fruit world, it needs virtually no pruning, is fully hardy and produces bucket loads of uniquely flavoured fruit, great for crumbles and pies – and don't bother removing the stones. If you're short of space grow one on your boundary as they survive in the hedgerows in the wild. *Merryweather* is a self-fertile variety.

Cherries are hardy and have lovely blossom but are only worth planting if you intend to employ a full-time bird-scarer!

'In an orchard there should be enough to eat, enough to lay up, enough to be stolen, and enough to rot on the ground.'
JAMES BOSWELL

Defining idea...

WELL-TRAINED FRUIT

Horticultural developments mean that you can now buy apples and pears that have been trained to specific shapes. Cordons grow at a 45° angle, while espaliers have a main vertical stem with horizontal tiers. Both are great space savers and can be grown against a wall or along a wire frame.

Step-over apples are espalier trees with the upward growth pruned out above the first set of horizontal branches, and provide excellent low 'walls' around the vegetable garden. Espaliers too can be used as decorative, productive screens.

Yep, there's a lot to take in with fruit trees, but just remember, there are few sweeter tastes than a ripe pear – except perhaps a ripe pear that you've grown yourself.

How did it go?

Q   How do I know when the fruit is ripe enough to pick?

A   With apples and pears take the fruit in the palm of your hand and gently twist. If it parts company easily it's ripe. If it doesn't, don't force it, leave it for a few more days. With plums, pick one and cut it in two. If the flesh comes away easily from the stone pick all the plums that appear to be at this same stage.

Q   My crop of plums has been great but how do I deter the wasps from enjoying it?

A   A good tip is to throw any over-ripe or half-eaten plums well away from the tree so the wasps can feast in peace. Then pick the remaining fruit the moment it becomes ripe.

18

Blow the raspberries

Whatever your age, juicy, sweet berries are a summertime delight, but which types and varieties suit which garden? And can you really grow a blackberry without prickles?

The beauty of berries is that they provide a quick return after planting, but while strawberries, raspberries and blackberries share some common ground, such as a preference for moist, well-drained soil that's mildly acidic, their growing habits and cultivation techniques are all significantly different. So sit up, and pay attention at the back.

STRAWBERRIES

For some, strawberries are the ultimate summer fruit, the king of the berries, with a big, bold crop just asking to be eaten. To get the best from strawbs, plant them in July or August to fruit the following summer. 'Honeoye' and 'Eros' are good all-rounders, while 'Cambridge Favourite' crops well, and is disease resistant.

Here's an
idea for
you...

If you can group all your berries together with other soft fruit then it may be worth buying a fruit cage to protect the whole lot. You can splash out on one with a metal frame, or build your own from wood. Then cover it with black or green nets, with a 2cm mesh, available from any hardware store. Remove nets in winter to prolong their life. It might sound a bit OTT but there can be few more soul-destroying sights than a fruit bush stripped bare before you've had a chance to harvest.

The plants prefer an open sunny spot with plenty of space between them, and need to be kept well watered, especially in spring when the fruits are swelling.

To keep the berries off the ground, where they can fall prey to slugs or rot, surround the plants with straw (one of many theories behind the plant's name) or strawberry mats, making sure the ground is moist first. As a final deterrent, net them to protect from the birds. To help your plants overwinter, remove the straw once they've finished fruiting, take off the old leaves, feed and mulch with well-rotted manure or garden compost.

Strawberries are thoughtful plants, providing not only a juicy crop but next year's plants as well. These come in the form of runners – those long stems with small plants attached that shoot off from the main plant. Choose the strongest of these – those nearest the plant – push them into the soil or small pots of compost, securing each with a bent piece of wire. Keep them attached to the parent plant for six weeks to allow the roots to form, before cutting them loose and planting them out. Sadly this free service doesn't last forever and the main strawberry plants will need replacing every 3–5 years.

RASPBERRIES

This prickly customer is relatively easy to grow, crops best in full sun and can last up to 20 years.

Before planting dig a trench, fill it with plenty of muck and mix in an all-round fertiliser. As the canes grow, cover them at the base with compost or grass cuttings to keep in the moisture, making sure the soil you're covering is already damp. But while they mustn't be allowed to dry out, water-logging can be just as harmful.

IDEA 10, *Support network*, will tell you what to do with raspberry canes that can grow to 1.5m, while for details on growing gooseberries see IDEA 52, *Currant thinking* – it may sound bizarre but read it and you'll see why.

Try another idea...

Plant summer fruiting raspberries in autumn, feeding and mulching in spring. 'Julia' is a good disease-resistant variety, while 'Tulameen' is a heavy cropper with few spines. This type of fruit grows on last year's canes, so it's important to only prune those canes that have just fruited, leaving the ones that have grown this year to bear next year's fruit. The autumn varieties, such as 'Autumn Bliss', produce raspberries on the current year's canes, so all the canes can be cut down to the ground after fruiting.

BLACKBERRIES

Blackberries are one of the most abundant fruits in nature's larder and throughout September blackberrying is one of those few pastimes that seems to transcend all ages. Octogenarians enjoy scrambling through the brambles just as much as eight-year-olds, often attacking the bush with a vigour unseen since they last attended the January sales, walking sticks thrashing wildly in their haste to bag a free lunch.

Blackberries have been around for over 2000 years, for eating, for hedging and for medicinal purposes – creeping under a bramble bush was long considered a cure for rheumatism, boils

'I am never so utterly at peace as when blackberrying or looking for mushrooms.'
ALAN BENNETT

Defining idea...

81

and blackheads. They enjoy the same rich, moist soils as the other berries but are a little less fussy. Plant in the autumn and immediately cut the stems down to just one bud. Each year, once fruiting has finished, cut down the stems that have fruited to allow new ones to develop. Make this easy by separating out the stems as they grow and training them against a fence.

They live for 20 years or more, and there are several varieties, such as the vigorous *Bedfordshire Giant,* the more moderate black butte, or the hybrid berry, boysenberry.

How did it go?

Q   I like the idea of growing berries but I'm running out of space – what can I do?

A   *Unlike other berries, strawberries are happy growing in containers such as strawberry pots, hanging baskets and even growbags. This has the double advantage of keeping the fruit well off the ground and saving space. Line the pot first with plastic to save it drying out, add a few drainage holes, and feed every two weeks with tomato feed once they start cropping.*

Q   How can I make blackberrying more child friendly?

A   *You don't have to plant those tough brutes you see in the wild, with their vicious, spiky thorns. Developments have resulted in thornless varieties too that still provide shiny, black fruit. These include 'Lochness' or 'Oregon Thornless', which also has attractive foliage.*

19

To prune or not to prune

How often have you purposefully strode out into the garden, secateurs in hand, intent on tidying up a headstrong hydrangea or mutinous mahonia, yet when you get within a few paces, the doubts kick in? Where do I start? Is it the right time of year? Will I end up killing it?

Pruning isn't just about chopping the top off a plant that's too big. Get it right and you'll be rewarded with a plant that produces plenty of flowers and fruit, has a good shape, and is a lot less prone to disease. So, take a moment or two to learn the whys, whens and hows of basic pruning, and who knows, you might find it so much fun you take up topiary!

WHY PRUNE?

Mark cut his gardening teeth pruning a forsythia hedge for his Grandma. The mass of yellow flowers seemed to come back year after year, so she was happy enough,

Here's an idea for you...

Fancy your hand at topiary? Shaping box, or the evergreen shrub honeysuckle (*Lonicera nitida*), into balls is a good way to start but turning a plain conical evergreen into a spiral is simple and effective. Tie a piece of rope to the top and spiral it around the plant to the bottom. Now cut alongside the rope to mark the line of the spiral. Remove the rope and trim further into the spiral until the desired shape is achieved.

and so was he, with the fiver it cost her for his dextrous shearing.

Pruning inspires plants; it's a chemical thing that makes them grow back in a different way. It may be a bit of an oxymoron but cutting plants back hard will stimulate rapid growth.

The basic pruning set should include a good pair of secateurs (for cutting stems and twigs up to 1cm thick), a pruning saw (for smaller branches), loppers for any hard-to-reach tough stuff, and garden shears for trimming soft growth. Try tackling everything with the same pair of blunt kitchen scissors and you'll be rewarded with mashed stems and a nice line in blisters.

WHEN TO DO IT?

Most plants need an annual prune to keep them healthy and productive. Just removing dead wood and any stems that are rubbing against each other (so letting in disease) can give even the most dishevelled shrub a new lease of life. And a cut in the right place, at the right time, can encourage side shoots, fruiting spurs and flowers. When to carry this out depends on the plant and when it flowers or fruits. There's no short cut – to do it properly you need to read up on the plant. But if it is done correctly, it's one of those jobs that brings on a warm glow of self-congratulation.

Many roses, soft fruits and fruiting trees need pruning in the dormant season – that time when they're asleep, from autumn through to early spring. Trained fruit trees will need summer pruning as well to keep them in shape.

Shrubs, however, fall into two main groups and while it's not difficult, if you get it wrong, you'll have to wait another year to see any flowers. If the shrub flowers in spring, on branches grown in the previous year – forsythia is a typical example – prune it after flowering. If you mistakenly cut it hard back before flowering, you'll be taking out the stems that are covered in buds. (Sorry Grandma.)

The second group are shrubs that flower later in the year, on the current year's growth, such as buddleia. Pruning these in early spring will encourage them to produce fresh growth that will flower later that summer.

There is a third group – slow-growing shrubs that keep the same basic shape, e.g. magnolia, azaleas, witch hazel and the hardy hibiscus. Leave these alone except for the pruning out of dead or damaged wood.

Generally keep an eye on things and try to avoid drastic action where one minute your garden will be looking overgrown, the next bald! Again, the best approach is to consult a well-illustrated guide that demonstrates clearly the action you need to take. It needs to show the difference between end and side shoots, explain exactly where to make your cuts, and preferably have a picture of how the plant should look afterwards!

IDEA 22, *It's been a good year for the roses*, looks more closely at how to keep your shrub roses under control.

Try another idea...

'*All gardens, even the most native and naturalistic, benefit from the hand of an artful pruner. In this season, where the garden is poised for the green flood of springtime, remember that our gardens are co-creations, shared with mother earth. And like any good mother, she expects you to tidy up your room. Now get clipping!*'
TOM SPENCER (US gardening guru)

Defining idea...

85

Deadheading is a small job that makes a big difference. You'll reap the rewards in your containers and summer border, and if you're prepared to risk the odd mishap, it's a good way to get children involved too. Not only does it tidy things up but it also stops the plants putting their energy into producing unwanted seeds. Cut the flower back below the seedpod and you'll encourage it to concentrate its efforts on producing more flowers instead.

How did it go?

Q   **Some plants in my garden are looking leggy – the lavender in particular. Can I cut it down to the ground?**

A   *Unfortunately lavender doesn't re-grow from old wood so trim these plants annually in March, cutting back to 5–10cm from the base where new shoots should be visible. Do not cut back into old or bare wood. If the lavender is really bare at the bottom dig it up and replant it in a deeper hole. Better still, start again with new plants, by taking cuttings from your existing plants in September, before throwing them away.*

Q   **I have some tough pruning jobs ahead of me as several trees have got out of control. Will a pruning saw be strong enough for this work?**

A   *A pruning saw is only suitable for the twiggy branches of shrubs and young trees. For major tree pruning, get the experts in. Don't attempt tree surgery or you may end up needing some yourself. But only use a bona fide company.*

20

Shrubs

The backbone of the garden – but are they really that interesting?

Without shrubs a garden would have no form. While trees provide the focal points, and perennials and annuals give that zip and zest in spring and summer, it's the much-maligned shrub that provides the structure, and the stage, for other plants to strut their stuff.

But that's not to suggest that shrubs just perform a supporting role in the garden. They come in a remarkable variety of shapes, sizes and colours. Some do their bit in winter, others in spring, summer or autumn. Some are spiky, others are feathery, and others still are broad-leaved. And most have showy flowers too!

WHAT IS A SHRUB?

In simple terms, it's a woody plant that doesn't die down in the winter. Bushy, unlike the tree with its single trunk, it may loose its leaves and look half dead for part of the year but rest assured, when the time's right, it will burst back into life again.

Shrubs also have many uses. Their chunky growth can act as a windbreak for more tender plants, while in a border of spring and summer flowers, they can provide structure and colour as the plants around them die down.

But are you brave enough to plant a whole bed of shrubs? No, not the 'motorway style' planting so beloved of town planners, where a mass of impenetrable *Pyracantha* suffices for 'landscaping', but a bed where leaf shape, colour and flowers are blended to change with the seasons.

Here's an idea for you...

In this day and age the humble shrub is also a weapon in our on-going war against crime. A well placed *Berberis* or firethorn (*Pyracantha*) is as effective a burglar deterrent as you'll find. Thankfully the evergreen firethorn has more redeeming features than just razor-sharp thorns, such as creamy flowers and vivid berries. The variety Orange Charmer is also less prone to scab and its orange berries will only be attractive to the birds once all the red ones have been eaten!

SHRUBS FOR ALL SEASONS

In spring, after the bulbs have done their bit, the faithful forsythia and flowering currant (*Ribes*) take over, followed shortly by stunning magnolias, sweet scented lilac and broom.

In late spring and early summer the selection grows. *Potentilla*, with its pink, flame, yellow and white flowering varieties, is worthy of a special mention. It's tough and uncomplicated to grow, and flowers all summer long on attractive feathery leaves. And, although it has no scent, you can easily fool the nostrils by planting something more heavily scented nearby, such as mock orange (*Philadelphus*).

Towards the end of summer the 'grow anywhere' buddleia, or butterfly bush, starts to flower. A true survivor, it's colonised building sites, railway embankments and even clogged up gutters the length and the breadth of the country.

For something more linguistically challenging, try *Ceratostigma willmottianum*. Of medium height and covered with intense blue flowers, it's a shrub that does well at the front of a bed, and looks good alongside the hardy hibiscus.

There's more on shrubs with winter interest in IDEA 30, *Winter wonderland*, and IDEA 19, *To prune or not to prune*, helps guard against giving your shrubs the unkindest cut of all.

Try another idea...

As the garden begins to shut down, the winter shrubs take over. Winter sweet (*Chimonanthus praecox*) and Sweet box (*Sarcococca confusa*) have small flowers but fabulous scent. *Garrya elliptica* is worth growing for its amazing long catkins, and if you have acid soil and a sunny spot, then squeeze in a Chinese witch hazel (*Hamamelis mollis*), with its eye-catching golden yellow flowers and beautiful smell.

Berberis is both beautiful and prickly. It comes in many forms, with leaves of bright yellow, deep green, scarlet or wine, as well as evergreen, deciduous, dwarf and large varieties. What they all share is some of the most vicious and spiky leaves in the gardening world. But with its spring flowers, autumn colour and winter berries it's a perfect all-rounder for the shrub border.

TREAT 'EM MEAN, KEEP 'EM KEEN

Still think shrubs are boring? OK, how about this as a selling point? A bed of shrubs is perhaps the most efficient area of any garden. In spring and autumn feed and prune (don't forget to check which shrubs should be pruned when), add compost to the soil and generally tidy up. Job's a good 'un.

'Shrub is a lovely word, sliding between the teeth with a soft landing. Shrubs help to mould a garden, adding colour, shape, texture and fragrance, and complementing trees, bulbs, annuals and perennials.'
From *Shrubs For The Garden* by JOHN CUSHNIE

Defining idea...

Mind you, neglect your duties and things will soon get out of control.

Unlike annuals and perennials, shrubs take a while to get settled and spread out. This is where a little planning comes in. It pays to check a shrub's estimated spread and height, and try to visualise what it will look like in three years' time. If you have planted your shrubs too closely together, then they won't mind being moved in autumn or spring, as long as there's a good layer of compost in their new hole, and you water them in thoroughly.

How did it go?

Q I love the stunning colours of rhododendrons and azaleas but can I grow them with other shrubs?

A *Yes, if you garden on acid soil. Try to imitate the conditions of a woodland glade and match them up with other woodland plants – bluebells, ferns, heathers and hellebores. Remember some do have tree-like proportions. Choose some of the dwarf azaleas if your site is restricted and a little more open.*

Q How can I keep the shrub bed looking good throughout the year?

A *By not forgetting evergreens:* Escallonia, Euonymous, Mahonia, Eleagnus, Skimmia japonica, *holly (*Hedera*) and* Pieris, *for example. In sheltered southern areas you could try* Pittosporum, Choisya *('Sundance' is the golden form),* Convolvulus, Cistus *or* Hebes. *Some varieties of* Vibernum, Berberis *and* Daphne *are evergreen too, and you have the full range of dwarf or slow-growing conifers to choose from. A sample of all these will help hold the bed together all year.*

21

And so to bed ...

Traditionally summer bedding was planted en masse but (thankfully) there are more subtle uses for these bright, vibrant and vigorous plants.

We won't beat about the bush — bad bedding can be frightening. A garden festooned in a pink and purple flurry of busy lizzies and pansies is the visual equivalent of GBH. Yes, we know some people love it, and will also throw in a few salvias and French marigolds for good measure, but please, there are more refined ways to use bedding.

After all, bedding is any type of flowering plant used specifically to give a few months display of colour, usually in spring and summer. They're not all annuals, they're not all tender, and they're not all pink.

Here's an idea for you...

If you're sowing your annuals directly in the ground try starting with what's termed a 'stale' seed bed. Cultivate the soil a good couple of weeks before you intend to plant it up and then leave it, allowing any weed seeds in the soil to germinate. Hoe these off and you can sow your annuals in a weed-free bed. Of course some weeds will return, but your seeds will have a head start.

Take your hardy annuals such as love-in-a-mist (*Nigella*) and nasturtiums. These can be sown straight into a prepared seed bed (the packet will tell you when) and can put up with the cold. In fact, you can also sow hardy annuals like the Californian poppy (*Eschscholzia californica*) and cornflowers (*Centaurea cyanus*) in late summer, to bloom early the following season.

It's a good idea to sow seeds in specific shapes on the ground, so you know what are seedlings and what are weeds when it comes to hoeing. And sow a couple of each plant in a pot too, label it up and then when they sprout, you'll know what your seedlings should look like.

Your half-hardy annuals, however, like cosmos and salvia, curl up and die at the first sign of frost, so these need sowing indoors from January onwards. Keep them warm, prick them out into biodegradable pots, and once you've gradually hardened them off, they can be planted straight into the ground, pot and all. This means you won't disturb those precious roots, and the pot will just rot away, enriching your soil at the same time!

Begonias, pelargoniums and cannas are also often classed as bedding although these can be treated as half-hardy perennials if overwintered out of the reach of frost.

Bedding also comes as plugs, usually via mail order, which will need potting on and hardening off before planting out, and of course you can buy bedding plants that are already in flower. Buying petunias as plugs is a good idea as their seed is very small and tricky to handle.

Growing from seed is not only cheaper but also teaches you so much more about horticulture. IDEA 2, *Top seed*, should help you on your way.

Try another idea...

But a word of warning: while trays of bright bedding may be on sale as early as April, resist the temptation to buy them. You can't plant bedding until the last frost has been and gone, which could be as late as early June in some places. And it's never a good idea to buy plants until you're ready to put them in the ground. Leave them hanging around in their trays and they'll get straggly and pot-bound.

When it comes to planting out, give your bedding a good watering first so the root ball gets really moist. And, while you might be planting them in optimum midsummer conditions, don't just plonk bedding in anywhere. You need to prepare the soil as much for a pansy as you would any other plant and most bedding grows best in well-drained soil in a sunny part of the garden.

When planting go carefully as annuals are delicate things. Make sure the roots aren't cramped or twisted, and plant them to the same depth as the original soil mark on the stem. Give them a good watering in, and then deadhead regularly to prolong flowering.

Now our idea of a good bedding is an impulse purchase used to fill a particular gap that's appeared in the border, or to invigorate a slightly forlorn hanging basket or tub.

'Bedding is apt to get a bad name because of the wretchedly mindless examples we see in public places. But at home, it gives us wonderful scope for variety. Lively and not so much with a song in its heart but an uninhibited shout of joy.'
CHRISTOPHER LLOYD

Defining idea...

Bedding is an important part of succession planting and, personally speaking, looks so much better fitted into an existing border of shrubs and perennials rather than planted en masse, and on its own. It can take over where early flowering plants have been cut back, and shrubs and perennials have yet to do their bit. More subtle than the psychedelic carpet some gardeners prefer.

How did it go?

Q **Any suggestions for good bedding plants with a bit of height?**

A *Haven't you heard of sunflowers? Helianthus is just as much an annual as a low-growing lobelia. Love-lies-bleeding (Amaranthus caudatus) is a half-hardy annual that does well in borders, with its dangling flower tassels. The tobacco plant Nicotiana sylvestris is over 1m and Clarkia elegans and Sweet Williams (Dianthus barbatus) will reach 60cm plus, whilst half-hardy fuchsias and cannas provide bold upright features when surrounded by lower growing bedding.*

Q **What do I do with my half-hardy perennials once they've done their bit?**

A *You can cut back plants like pelargonium and chrysanthemums to just a few centimetres, dig them up, re-pot them, and overwinter in a frost-free place. But some experts say you'll get much better plants from cuttings taken in late summer. If you go down this route keep a regular eye on them, adjusting the humidity if necessary, to make sure they don't rot away.*

22

It's been a good year for the roses

Roses have made something of a comeback over recent years, although arguments still rage over their care, their cultivation and even their classification.

Now, in the interests of brevity and sanity, I'm not even going to attempt to cover the thorny area of rose nomenclature. Suffice to say the species behind this recent resurgence is wildly held to be the modern shrub rose.

Technically any rose bred after 1867 is considered modern, although given that the Crusaders were bringing back species from abroad as long ago as the thirteenth century, it does still make them reasonably novel.

What sets them apart from other roses is their breeding. It's their lineage that makes them so diverse, because not only do they draw on all the finer qualities of the older roses such as scent and vigour, but also characteristics of the modern species, such as long flowering periods (given some diligent deadheading), bright colours and disease resistance.

Here's an idea for you...

Don't fall foul of Rose Replant Disease! When replacing an old rose with a new one, make sure you dig out a good proportion of the old soil, to a depth and width of about 50–60cm. Replace it with soil that has never been near a rose. The reason for this is that all roses have a fungus on their roots and the soil around them, which seems to be harmless to the old plant, can be overwhelming for new plants, and weakens them before they get going.

Defining idea...

'There has been a huge swing away from the sort of roses my grandparents loved, fancy Hybrid Teas and Florinbundas with names like 'Tallyho' and 'Gay Gordons'. In summer, borders glowed like Las Vegas, in winter they looked like the Somme.'
STEPHEN LACEY

Of course, roses are renowned for their beauty, the exquisite composition of their foliage, their scent and the velvety texture of their petals, but modern shrub roses are also wonderfully informal plants, which suits the current vogue for naturalistic planting. After all, what would you choose to complement your carefully planted border – a large flowered Hybrid Tea, pruned and clipped within an inch of its life, or the branching stems and dripping flower clusters of a modern shrub rose?

That said, they can be sprawling beasts, with some capable of forming mounds more than 2m high, such as R. 'Nevada', which produces creamy white flowers on arching stems.

Others make excellent hedges, such as R. 'Buff Beauty', with its large clusters of apricot flowers, and R. 'Cornelia', with apricot-pink flowers set against dark green leaves.

As for colour, R. 'Ethelburga' is a new variety with highly scented pink flowers, while R. 'Autumn Sunset' is a deep yellow, with bright glossy foliage.

A few tips on planting roses in general. During the growing season they can be bought in containers. But buying them as bare-rooted plants, during the dormant season is generally a cheaper and healthier option.

IDEA 47, *Common diseases* considers some of the ailments that could strike your plants.

Try another idea...

You need to add plenty of compost or well-rotted manure to the planting hole, making sure that the soil has a neutral pH. They will do much better in a sunny site but mulch regularly to keep the roots moist.

Modern shrub roses don't need extensive pruning. In spring, remove any dead or diseased wood, and then cut back the main shoots by about a third and any side shoots by about two thirds. They do need staking, however, and tough metal rings are required to keep them shapely and their flowers off the ground.

As for diseases, modern shrubs are more resistant than many varieties to the usual suspects such as mildew, black spot and rose rust but, as with all roses, good cultivation is the best way to fend off pests and diseases.

'What place, I often ask myself, should roses take in our gardens? A silly question, really, because each of us has to make up his mind about it for himself and each will reach a different conclusion, right for him, wrong for his neighbour.'
CHRISTOPHER LLOYD

Defining idea...

OK, having said I'm not going to get bogged down in classifications, special mention is due to *R. rugosa*, or the Japanese rose. It's a close relation of the modern shrub and considered by some to be the healthiest of all roses, doing well in most soils and vigorous enough to make excellent hedges. *Scabrosa* has unusual, velvety, mauve flowers and a flush of huge red hips in autumn, while for scent try the pure white R. 'Blanche Double de Coubert'.

Q   Cut the wise cracks – but what's a sucker?

A   *Most roses you plant in your garden have been budded or grafted onto rootstock from a wild rose to give it extra vigour, among other things. A sucker is any shoot that's growing from below where your cultivated rose has been added. Ignore them and the wild variety will soon take over. But don't prune them off, suckers need to be pulled off, moving some of the top soil to get at them.*

Q   I know you don't want to talk species and classification but what's the difference between a climber and a rambler?

A   *Ramblers are unruly but gloriously effervescent, clothing structures with rapid growth and showers of smallish flowers. Climbers are more restrained and dignified, featuring spaced out larger blooms on fewer but thicker stems. It's a question of horses for courses.*

23

If it's good enough for pandas

From the wild jungles of China to the elegance and solitude of a classic Japanese garden, the versatility – and occasionally the roots – of bamboo knows no bounds.

Mark remembers a bamboo in the back garden of the house he grew up in. And also how exotic it seemed to have something growing in North London that was surely more at home in the jungle. He even had fanciful ideas that a distant relative, a captain in the Merchant Navy perhaps, had brought it back from China. But it was more likely won at the local church bazaar.

ME OLD BAMBOO

While the bamboo may originate in far-off, exotic climes, there are over 200 temperate varieties that grow happily in the UK. After all, this is a plant that's perfectly at home in

Here's an idea for you...

One of the great benefits of a tall, mature bamboo is that it makes an instant screen, and can help blot out an eyesore that may otherwise ruin the effect of the garden. Although not cheap to buy, mature bamboo does establish well. When buying, generally the more canes on a clump the better.

the Himalayas, and laughs in the face of the worst Jack Frost can throw at it.

Bamboos are grasses with woody stems and lush, usually evergreen, leaves. They can grow to just 10cm – or to 10m plus – and have canes, or culms, that vary from gold through to black, forming tight clumps or spreading out over a huge area. Some can be used as ground cover, other as screens, and they're also popular for their swaying and constant movement.

Bamboo differs from other plants in a number of ways. For a start, when a cane emerges, it will, unlike a tree, retain the same girth and never thicken. It will also reach its full height in one year. New, thicker, more vigorous, taller clumps will flow as the roots get stronger. Branches and leaves grow from the nodes on the canes. But it's the roots or rhizomes that cause all the problems. Some species can grow up to a metre a day, but while you need to be cautious with bamboo, there are plenty of clump forming varieties that are easily kept in check.

That said, when planting all but the smallest clump forming varieties, it pays to surround the plant with an impenetrable barrier of thick plastic, or metal, buried two or three feet down. (This barrier needs a bottom to it as, if the sides are blocked, the rhizomes will grow downwards.) This will stop the roots running and taking over the garden. Most enjoy well-drained soil and a sunny site and, once planted, need very little care – bar the odd bit of pruning in spring to thin out old and dead canes. Old leaves and their sheaths should be left around the base of the plant as a mulch.

Of course, you don't grow bamboo for its flowers. As a result the best way to propagate bamboo is through division. If you do manage to coax yours into flower you could do the plant more harm than good, as producing the grass-like heads can exhaust them. This is why some species flower once every 100 years but incredibly, if one species does flower, it's likely to do so all over the world that year.

IDEA 44, *Whispering grass don't tell the trees*, and IDEA 50, *Frills and fronds*, will give you some inspiration for planting schemes using complementary leaf shapes.

Try another idea...

Here are four varieties, all with different habits, that you may want to try in your garden.

- **Dwarf white-striped bamboo** (*Pleioblastus variegates*). A good bamboo for the beginner that grows to about 75cm. It also spreads slowly, which makes it compact enough for a small garden or container. The leaves are variegated green and cream, and it works particularly well with other grasses or taller bamboos. Cut back the old culms in spring.
- **Umbrella bamboo** (*Fargesia murieliae*). This is one of the most widely grown bamboos and another one that suits the beginner. It grows to around 4m and doesn't mind heavy, clay soil. It produces tall clumps of green canes, which often arch under the weight of its own apple-green leaves. Perfect as a screen or wind break.
- **Black Bamboo** (*Phyllostachys nigra*). Very de rigueur at the moment but not the easiest to grow. Can reach between 3–5m, with slender canes that turn jet black after a couple of years. This is a great plant for round the pond (although not with its roots in water) as it produces some beautiful reflections.

'Bamboos are an easy way to mimic a garden Paradise.'
MONTY DON

Defining idea...

■ **Fishpole Bamboo** (*Phyllostachys aurea*). This can get big and grow well over 5m, with grooved, and often distorted, brown-yellow canes and golden-green leaves. Where it really wins though is that it's one of the least invasive on the market.

How did it go?

Q Not very well, now you ask. I planted a bamboo a few years back and it's taken over the whole border. Help! What can I do?

A *Don't panic, and don't reach for the weedkiller either. Despite having rampant roots, the bamboo's rhizomatous roots are actually quite shallow. This means you can dig them out, although you need to get every bit to stop it growing back.*

Q Any varieties that should be avoided?

A *There are a few, such as* Sasa plamata, *which is particularly rampant, and you should think carefully before planting any of the* Pleioblastus *varieties, which will run wild!*

Q Can I grow bamboo in a pot?

A *Good idea but you've got to be prepared to keep potting it on and dividing it every few years, or it could burst out! Never let it dry out either, and a bit of slow-release fertiliser in the soil will help it along. Let its own leaves do the mulching.*

24

Oh I do like to be beside the seaside

Sand, salt and sea don't sound like a great combination when it comes to a garden but you'll be amazed at what you can grow beside the seaside.

There are two big problems with gardening on the coast: salt and wind. Salt dehydrates plants, while the wind will decimate what's left.

Yet despite this, there's a surprisingly large range of plants that can be grown by the coast, especially if windbreaks such as hedges or filter fences are used to reduce the force of the wind, and stop some of the salty spray hitting your plants.

First, a few tips. As a general rule, look out for plants with small leaves, which do better in a coastal setting. Equally, plants with grey, furry leaves such as phlomis are a good buy. These can withstand the salt much better than most other plants, as the small hairs keep the salt away from the surface of the leaf.

Another clue is in the plant's name. If it has *maritimum* or *littoralis* after it then it's a plant that comes from the coast, and one which should be happy in your garden.

Here's an idea for you...

One of the great benefits of a seaside garden is that the warming influence of the sea means it won't suffer from severe and heavy frost. So, with a bit of shelter, it's possible to grow perennials and exotics that wouldn't fare so well inland. These include many architectural plants such as cistus, cannas and cordylines.

As for windbreaks, evergreen escallonias are a good choice, with dark, glossy leaves which are able to withstand the salt, while pink or red flower clusters brave the elements intermittently from early summer onwards. Hebes can also put up with the salt-laden wind, as can the feathery foliage of *Tamarix tetandra*.

Hedges have a bit more give than solid garden walls, which can actually channel the wind straight into the very beds you are trying to protect. You can also catch glimpses of the landscape through a hedge, or actually use them to frame a view.

Defining idea...

'The artichoke outside my window has fourteen buds and is shoulder high, the huge thistles have filled out, the roses are in full leaf, the sages are in bud, the everlasting peas sprawl around lazily across the shingle. The gorse, which took a battering, is sprouting.'
From *Derek Jarman's Garden*

And so to the plants. The Sea holly (*Eryngium maritimum*) throwing up spiny blue-grey bracts from June through to September, really is as tough as it looks and makes an excellent foil for other plants.

Red-hot pokers (*Khiphofia*) are another good seaside choice. Try growing a small variety such as Little Maid, which can stand up to the worst the weather can hurl at it. It's also long flowering with ivory blooms tipped with yellow from June until the end of August.

The tree lupin (*Lupinus arboreus*) is an evergreen perennial that thrives in sandy conditions. If it dies after a few years don't worry, they are short lived but it will be well worth investing in another. They have spikes of pale-yellow scented flowers, and are a great shrub for offering shelter to other more tender plants.

Other candidates include sea lavender (*Limonium latifolium*), thrift (*Armeria*), chamomile (*Anthemis*) and the low-growing, mat-forming sedums, as well as Mediterranean herbs such as rosemary and thyme.

Cyclamen grow wild along the coast and are easily cultivated in the seaside garden, and the white rambling rose, Seagull, with its stiff, strong shoots, also does well.

One of the UK's most famous seaside gardens belonged to the late painter and filmmaker Derek Jarman. He turned a stretch of shingle beach in the lee of Dungeness power station, in Kent, into a magical space full of weird, spiky plants. One of his favourites was sea kale (*Crambe maritime*) with its fleshy blue-green, sometimes purple leaves. They die away completely in winter before sprouting again in March, the beaches' first sign that spring is on the way.

But, just like gardens in the city or the countryside, no two seaside gardens are the same. For every Jarmanesque homage to

Supporting your plants in a windy garden is vital, so check out IDEA 10, *Support network*.

Try another idea...

'Isn't it better to produce a garden that looks at home in the reality of your climate, than to plant a garden full of flapping exotics and see them suffer? A garden full of war-zone plants, plants that are just getting by, is not a recipe for a relaxing garden, visually or physically.'
STEPHEN ANDERTON

Defining idea...

pebbles and stones, there's another plot hanging on to the top of a cliff, or another surrounding a bungalow in a small seaside town. What they do share is a setting which at times is all tranquillity and peace, yet at others foreboding and hostile.

How did it go?

Q   I fancy a tree in my seaside garden. Would I be wasting my time?

A   *Choose carefully. There are a few trees that will put up with a constant coating of saline spray, such as the tough old sycamore. Yew is tolerant of thin soils, drought and exposure and the ash is also good on exposed sites, although they're large hungry trees and little will grow under them.* Sorbus aria, *with its crimson berries, also does well.*

Q   Any ideas for introducing some much needed annual colour to my seaside garden?

A   *With a bit of shelter and a sunny spot, cornflowers, poppies and daisies all spring to mind. Echiums cope well with sandy, chalky soil, and have a range of colours from white through to purple. They also make a good plant for ground cover. The wild flower, viper's bugloss (*E. vulgare*), is the most recognisable.*

106

25

Red alert – with a touch of orange, yellow, amber ...

It's not just the trees and shrubs that add autumn colour to the garden; there are plenty of perennials and bulbs that can bring some seasonal dazzle to the borders.

Some gardeners disappear into their own terracotta shell as the leaves begin to fall. They may occasionally be seen shuffling around the potting shed or berating the postman when their seed catalogue still hasn't arrived, but generally they tend to enter the equivalent of horticultural hibernation.

Yet, should they dare to venture outside, there's a phenomenal range of plants that keep interest going in the garden until the first frosts and beyond. And they'd probably be surprised to hear that they're available in more than just shades of red.

Here's an idea for you...

Seed-heads can also add interest and colour to the post-summer garden, so it pays to leave on some of the more majestic. The Chinese lantern (*Physalis alkekengi*) looks good in the borders or in tubs, while a frosted thistle or teasel is a dramatic sight in the misty morning light. And don't dismiss the humble rose hip, either.

PERENNIAL PERFORMERS

Some of our most recognisable plants come into their own during the autumn. To get the most from them, you need to give a bit of thought to where you plant them, and what other flowers or foliage will be peeking up as they come through.

A great autumn stalwart is the aster, or Michaelmas daisy, which like many of the daisy-shaped flowers is an import from the North American prairies. The rivalry in aster circles reads like the plot from a 1980s soap, with the New York asters (*A. novi-belgii*) vying for top notch with the New England asters (*A. novae-angliae*). The latter tends to win out, with more flowers and paler foliage. Try the large mauve flowers of *A.* 'Mrs S.T. Wright', or the rose-pink *A.* 'Harrington's Pink'.

Asters like the sun, with their roots in well-drained, fertile soil, and should be cut back to ground level and mulched as soon as they've done their bit.

Another plant with its roots in the prairies is the rudbeckia. Again, there's a myriad of types, and it's easily grown from seed, as one of us recently found out with an innocent packet of *R.* 'Rustic Dwarf'. They just kept on sprouting and the mahogany, amber and gold flowers couldn't be given away for love or money in the end. A larger variety is *R.* 'Herbstsonne', with floppy golden petals up to 10cm across.

Sedums offer a completely different colour palate to rudbeckias, with pinks, mauves and purples. Also known as the iceplant because their leaves are cold to the touch, they offer up flat flower heads much loved by any surviving autumnal bees, although they also pay a passing resemblance to some hybridised version of pink broccoli. This is another plant that likes a sunny, fertile, well-drained spot, but which also benefits from a bit of support come mid-summer. The rust-coloured 'Autumn Joy' (*S.* 'Herbstfreude') and the mauve *S.* 'Spectabile' are probably the most common and *S.* 'Purple emperor' with dark purple leaves and a mass of small pink flower heads is a welcome new addition. Iceberg is one of the most spectacular.

IDEA 5, *Indian summer* **looks at how to get the most from summer flowering plants, while there's much talk of fiery foliage with IDEA 43,** *Small trees for small gardens.*

Try another idea...

Other perennials worthy of a mention at this time of year are free-flowering hardy chrysanthemums, the dainty rose-pink South African lily (*Schizostylis*) and clump-forming Japanese anemone. The pink form looks great against a background of Firetail (*Persicaria amplexicaulis*), and the white on its own, or amongst dark-green foliage.

AUTUMN BULBS

There are plenty of autumn bulbs too, which should be planted in the spring. *Nerine bowdenii*, with its large clusters of pink lily-like flowers, is excellent in a sheltered sunny spot, at the base of a wall. Crocuses also pop their heads up in autumn, including *C. speciosus*, with its many hybrids such as the dark violet 'Oxonian' and the pure white 'Album', that look good

'As summer edges into autumn the oranges can mass slightly, chrysanthemums, dahlias, gladioli and red-hot pokers rudely milling in amongst the effete garden party.'
MONTY DON

Defining idea...

naturalised in grass. There are also colchicums, similar to crocus but with oval-shaped corms. These are ideally planted in groups in semi-shade among the shrubs. And for a burst of yellow in September/October, try *Sternbergia lutea*, which as you'd expect, loves full sun.

Add to all this a backdrop of reddening trees and shrubs, swaying grasses, frosted seed-heads and the odd shot of evergreen foliage, and even the most reclusive autumnal gardener will be forced to poke his head from underneath his shell.

Q   **No sooner had I planted some Michaelmas daisies than the old chap next door starting going on about mildew. Is he right?**

A   *'Miserable dark foliage, invariably adorned with mildew,' is how one learned gardening writer describes the New York asters. Try the New England varieties instead. They're more resistant. But mildew can also be a sign that your plants need more water, more feed and even dividing up.*

Q   **I've got good autumn colour but nothing with berries on. Any suggestions?**

A   *For a bold statement of intent try* Callicarpa bodinieri *with its fantastic violet berries. There's a wide range of cotoneasters that are heavily laden with berries, usually red, in the autumn, as well as the firethorn, Pyracantha, with red- and orange-berried varieties, and over 450 varieties of berberis to choose from, many festooned in seasonal berries. Those that are deciduous have stunning autumn foliage too.*

26

Cutting a dash

Some long leggy blooms were just made for the vase but how do you get your supermodels to look their best before their time in the spotlight?

Gardening is many things to many people. Some go in for monster veg, others see a perfect lawn as the pinnacle of their achievements, others decide to specialise in a particular species such as conifers or grasses. But for most gardening is about colour — and that means flowers.

The trick is to be able to provide fresh cut blooms for the house without denuding the garden. But don't ignore other garden highlights such as autumn fruits, striking leaves, coloured stems and even bare twigs, which all have their part to play.

A CUT ABOVE THE REST

Many plants do well when cut including wild hedgerow flowers, shrubs and tree prunings, but perennials and annuals are the showiest.

Here's an idea for you...

Bring spring forward a few weeks by cutting some forsythia twigs at the end of February. Choose branches that are covered in flower buds (although these will still be closed) and put them in a vase on a light windowsill. In a week or so they'll open and you can enjoy bright yellow blossom at least three weeks before it appears outside. Amelanchier branches will also do the business.

As a guide, in spring choose newly emerging blossom or the first spring flowers such as daffodils, bluebells and tulips. Try a few stems of lily-of-the-valley in a small glass too.

In summer you can select almost anything from the border, and use shrubs for a bit of bulk. The Peruvian lily (*Alstroemeria*) makes a great cut flower but can be tricky to get going. Buy them in pots with the leaves just beginning to show as it's difficult to get the bare roots into growth. Plant in full sun, in the middle of the border and don't move. Perhaps the best summer flowers for picking – indeed they should be picked every other day – are sweet peas (*Lathyrus odorataus*). Choose a scented variety such as Painted Lady or Fragrantissima. Dig a deep pit, add a generous layer of compost, backfill and plant against supports. Once the blooms appear pick, pick and pick again unless you want a tripod of peas instead of flowers!

There's plenty of colour in autumn too. Make sure you have dahlias and daisies in your border, such as rudbeckia, Michaelmas daisies and helenium. The vibrant and vigorous firetail (*Persicaria amplexicaulis*) grows like a weed throughout summer and autumn, but it's great for filling out large arrangements. And at this time of year you can add interest with rose hips, honeysuckle berries and clematis seed-heads.

Even in winter there are still plenty of possibilities for the vase. Catkins (*Corylus avellana*) and pussy willow (*Salix caprea*) are starting to show – as are snowdrops, which can tough out the most severe winter. Pick hellebores too – as they look great close up – but 'sear' the stems after picking to prevent them flopping. And where would we be without holly (*Ilex*) and ivy (*Hedra*) for a touch of festive cheer. To ensure holly keeps its berries for the end-of-year celebrations, pick it early before the birds get to it. Stick the stems in a patch of soil and protect them with a plastic bag.

IDEA 2, *Top seed*, demystifies growing plants from seed, and IDEA 20, *Shrubs*, may whet your appetite for flowering shrubs.

Try another idea...

Tempting though they may be, don't bring hawthorn or gelder rose blossom indoors as they smell of Tom cats, and wear gloves when cutting *Euphorbia* as the sap can cause irritation.

CUTTING EDGE

If you're really keen, and never want to have to buy in flowers again, then why not develop a separate 'cutting garden'. Include bulbs and favourite perennials, together with scented climbers and small flowering trees. If space is restricted, then pinch a corner of the veg patch.

Plant lots of annuals, choosing a mixture of colours and shapes, like cosmos, clarkia, marigolds (*Calendula*), snap dragons (*Antirrhinums*), cornflower (*Centaurea*), love-in-a-mist (*Nigella*) and tobacco plants (*Nicotiana*). Sow in seed trays in the spring and transplant once the last frosts have gone.

Prepare the soil well by adding compost and a sprinkle of bonemeal, and plant in rows or clumps for a bit of mutual support – but make sure you've room to pick them. Once the performance starts, add a bit more support, give some liquid feed and water well.

'There's nothing like going out into the garden and picking flowers for the house. It's the gardener's equivalent of collecting new-laid eggs from nesting boxes.'
SARAH RAVEN

Defining idea...

BLOOMING GOOD

To get the best out of cut flowers there are some simple rules. Cut at an angle, for maximum intake of water, remove lower leaves and place in tepid water as soon as possible. Crush woody stems and slit tough stalks to encourage them to take up water. Any flowers that leak sap or are flopping can be sealed and brought back to life by dipping the stems in boiling water for 20 secs. For a lasting effect add some 'cut flower food' to the water, or a teaspoon of sugar mixed with a few drops of bleach, and keep the vase away from heat.

How did it go?

Q **When I cut roses for the house they either droop straight away or fail to open at all. What should I do?**

A *Not all varieties behave well when cut. Those that do include Iceberg (white), New Dawn (pale pink), Graham Thomas (yellow) or Charles de Mills (deep red). The old fashioned rose, Rosa Mundi (Rosa gallica vesicular), does well too and has stunning hips in autumn. Cut your chosen stems whilst still in bud and make a 2cm slit up each stalk, to increase the take up of water.*

Q **Having grown flowers for cutting do I need flower-arranging classes?**

A *Although formal arrangements have their place, don't feel under pressure to create a work of art. A natural group in a jug will do fine. You'll need to collect a choice of containers over time but for starters a pale green vase, 25cm tall, will set off most flowers and branches well ... and you'll need a small glass container for the sweet peas.*

27

Hedging your bets

Hedges are a long-term project but there's a lot to be gained from planting a wall of box or yew.

Not too long ago farmers were ripping up hedges by the kilometre in an attempt to win ever more land for cultivation. Gardeners, whether consciously or not, appeared to follow suit, driven by the need to keep up with the Joneses and their latest in wavy lap larch board, classic picket, or rustic post and pole fences. Fortunately, the trend has been bucked.

Unless you've inherited a hedge that happens to be in the right place, establishing a new one takes some years. So why do you want a hedge? Is it purely a decorative feature, or are you looking to create a screen to ensure some privacy and cut out noise? Perhaps you want to establish a boundary, need a windbreak, or simply want to attract wildlife?

Here's an idea for you...

An unlikely candidate for hedging is buddleia, but if you're not a stickler for hedges clipped to perfection then create a 'buddleia barrier' for summer and autumn. Then it's great for that wispy, shaggy look, while its colourful, vibrant flowers are the perfect lure for butterflies.

A mixed, informal hedge covers most options (whisper it, but we're covering conifers later). Hazel, hawthorn, beech and hornbeam are some of the most common.

It's essential to plant up a new hedge in the late autumn, as the plants will need time to find their feet before the first growing period the following spring. Apart from the usual organic matter, some bonemeal will help them on their way. These first six months are the most critical period, so water at the first sign of a dry spell and resist the urge to clip them, however unkempt their appearance.

Should you be the proud owner of an already established but unruly mixed hedge, give some serious thought to laying it. There's evidence that this ancient country craft is enjoying something of a revival, so here's your chance to make a contribution. The end product provides you with a windbreak, screen and a haven for birds.

It's a job best done in the late winter or early spring, just as the sap is beginning to rise. If your hedge is on a slope start at the bottom and work up, otherwise start at either end. Use a billhook to chop the trunks almost through. This is lighter and sharper than an axe, and the chopping action will cut through any branch quickly and easily. Now more pliable, push them over, laying them up the slope at an angle of about 40°. As you move along, drive in rough-hewn stakes at 1m intervals, and then weave and intertwine the leaning branches between the stakes.

If you can, to give everything a bit more rigidity, thread willow wands and hazel rods between and along the hedge top. Both these and the stakes will rot away in time, and by then the hedge will have thickened enough to support itself.

Privet will grow anywhere and if you want to discover the artist in you, use it for some topiary. See IDEA 19, *To prune or not to prune*.

Try another idea...

You can trim the hedge when you've finished but not necessarily to spirit-level accuracy. Perhaps better to let nature take its course instead, with her characteristic undulations.

Bear in mind, though, that you need to let your newly planted hedge settle in for a few years before laying.

PINES NEEDLE

Ok, here we go, can't put it off any longer. The conifer: it's suffered in recent years, thanks largely to those leylandii innocently planted in the 1970s, which have now reached maturity. They're a suburban blight, and as a result the popularity of all conifers seems to have plummeted to such an extent that you're now more likely to read about them in the law courts section of your daily paper, rather than the gardening pages.

'... shaping a hedge is the closest most of us will ever come to doing sculpture or erecting a monument, but I think the real reward is more mundane. Shearing is very empowering – it gives you an exhilarating sense of control and achievement. You can stand back afterward and say, "look what I've done".'
From *All About Hedges* by RITA BUCHANAN

Defining idea...

117

In the right place, a conifer hedge does still have a lot going for it – all you need to do is monitor it closely and make sure it's kept at a manageable height.

There are two essentials you need to consider first. Proportion – if you've got 10,000sqm to play with then the sky's the limit, but in a small garden the last thing you want is a hedge soaring 20ft up in the air, blocking out all your light, with thirsty roots turning the ground beneath it into a dust bowl.

The other essential, if your hedge is part of the boundary between yourself and the neighbours, is to let them know first. It can avoid so much hassle in the future.

If time is on your side try yew, which is a relatively slow grower. Given acid to neutral free-draining soil it will add 30cm a year, but it does give the richest of greens and is one of the few evergreens that allows you to prune back into old wood. In a hurry? Cypress (especially *Chamaecyparis lawsoniana*) is a speed merchant growing at 1m a year!

Other shrubs not normally associated with hedges, but which perform perfectly well, are the ornamental plum (*Prunus cerasifera*) or the purple berberis (*B. thunbergii*) – the thorns of the latter will also deter intruders. The thick evergreen *Escallonia macrantha* will help maintain your privacy.

Of course, fences have their place but gardens are about living, natural things. And you can add more life and colour to your hedge by encouraging other plants to grow through it. Honeysuckle's the leading contender along with varieties of rose and clematis, while it's not uncommon for a blackberry bush to self seed and put in a welcome appearance.

Q   Box – it's a bit overrated isn't it?

A   Box is at its best when given a short back and sides. Keep it low and smart, and it makes an ideal frame for vegetables, or to give shape to groups of annuals or perennials.

Q   I thought my plants would be protected in the lee of my new hedge, but they actually seem to be suffering. Why is this?

A   Hedges are greedy bruisers and consume all available surrounding water. Keep your hedge trimmed so it is narrower rather than wider at the top, and place your plants at least a metre away from its base, where they will seek their own moisture and still enjoy the shelter of the hedge.

How did it go?

28

On the waterfront

Whether you're using the latest in toughened liners or an old washing-up bowl, ponds add a whole new aspect and lease of life to the garden.

In Europe the humble pond dates back to medieval times. The cloistered walks of abbeys and monasteries often included a well or fountain to aid meditation, while in Renaissance Italy they took on an altogether different look.

Along with fountains they became big, brash and ornate, the central feature of a wave of formal gardens sweeping across Europe. By the time Versailles was built in 1715, size was everything, and a fountain was considered inadequate if its jet was anything less than 100ft.

It took the sober British to bring things back down to earth, as the Romantic period took hold, and nature came back into vogue. But enough of the history. The point is that, while ponds are a fantastic addition to any garden, size really does matter.

Defining
idea...

'The still surface of the pool reflects the ever-changing patterns of the clouds, and the broad stone surround invites you to sit and let your tensions slip away.'
GEOFF HAMILTON

A pond wouldn't be complete without waterlilies (*Nymphaea*) and, as well as stunning flowers, their broad leaves help shade the pond and reduce green algae. N. *pygmaea* is ideal for small ponds, N. *alba* and the crimson N. *Escarboucle* are vigorous if you're looking for something bigger. They're best grown in baskets, which have been lined with an old sack to stop the soil escaping. Use heavy garden soil, top out with gravel and then sit them at the recommended depth.

Oxygenating plants are essential – but once established they can be invasive, so during the summer be brutal and remove plenty. *Elodea crispa* is the most manageable.

POOL MAINTENANCE

Shading the surface of your pond from direct sunlight with surface plants or overhanging trees will help the water stay clear and algae free. But net the pond in autumn to prevent dead leaves falling in and contaminating the water.

Installing a small pump will help keep the water aerated and grace your pond with either a fountain or trickle feature. Electrics are required here and must be handled by a professional. Clean and check the pump once a year.

Submerge a stocking packed with barley straw to combat blanket weed – believe us you'll experience this sooner or later. It may be an old wives' tale but usually has some impact. Pull the green cobweb-like weed out whenever you can too, and leave it on the side for a day so any small water creatures can crawl back into the pond.

Q **I'm embarrassed to say that my butyl liner is showing – what's the remedy?**

How did it go?

A *Assuming the top of the pond is level, and you really did use a spirit level during construction, try surrounding the pond, or just those exposed areas, with flattish stones. Lay them so they hang over the pond's edge to hide any lining. You can even firm them in with a few blobs of mortar but leave the occasional, strategically placed gap on the shallow side for frogs to escape.*

Q **The pond freezes over in winter, sometimes for several weeks. Does this matter?**

A *For that length of time, yes, as the water needs oxygen. When freezing weather is forecast leave an old football in the pond. It will help you create a breathing hole each day. But never smash the ice with an axe or sledgehammer as the shock waves will kill fish, frogs and newts.*

29

Danger – children at play

Children and gardens don't always mix, but there are ways of making a garden fun for kids without turning it into a council playground.

Clumsiness, carelessness and the odd bit of blundering, well they're just part of growing up, aren't they? Broken plates, absent-minded doodling on the wall, a large red stain on the hall carpet. Hey, who cares?

It's when this bungling is transferred to the garden that tensions can be strained, because while carpets can be cleaned and walls scrubbed, prize winning blooms are irreplaceable, for a year at least.

But if you're a gardener with kids then you'll want them outside, taking an intcrest in flowers, nature and the environment.

Here's an idea for you... **The stark A-frame of a swing can jar in a garden. But look again, and with some carefully positioned twine and the odd stick, you've got the perfect support for climbers like clematis, honeysuckle and sweet pea. A plant in each corner, and suddenly your kids have a leafy swing and you have a garden feature.**

KINDERGARTEN

First things first, kids love to dig, so to avoid them excavating what to young eyes may look like a bare patch of ground, but which is actually a seed bed raked to a fine tilth, leave a patch for them.

If they're old enough, encourage them to grow something; if not, just let them use it as a dumping ground, somewhere to empty and bury things before the joy of rediscovery.

Kids need easy-to-grow, tough, resistant plants that, nine times out of ten, do exactly what it promises on the packet. Many of the large seed companies now produce a special range of annuals for children.

You can't go wrong with the bright colours of sunflowers – with the annual competition to grow the tallest – marigolds, cornflowers, campanula and pansies. They'll also love fluffy Lamb's ears and nasturtiums.

Edible things in the garden are also a plus, and can teach an important lessons about which plants can be eaten and which can't. Strawberries grown in hanging baskets make for an interesting and tasty treat, as do crispy green runner beans, sweet pod fresh peas and crunchy carrots (although these will need a wash). Herbs are a winner too – easy to grow, great to smell, and good to eat.

Attracting wildlife into the garden is another way of firing young imaginations. The more organic your garden, the more beetles, bees and butterflies that are likely to live there. And you won't have to worry about kids touching leaves sprayed with pesticides, or picking up intriguing blue slug pellets.

However, short of discovering a pride of lions behind the potting shed, even wildlife will only hold the attention for so long. Garden toys are also required.

The most avant-garde designer would struggle to find a place for sandpits and trampolines in a garden, but even these can be disguised with a bit of hard graft, that great gardening euphemism for digging. In this case you're burying the aforementioned toys: putting the trampoline into a pit, with the bouncy bit at ground level, and building a simple sunk brick pit with a lid for the sand. Out of sight, out of mind?

NATURE'S TOYS

There are countless other ideas too. You can use willow whips to make living wigwams and tunnels. Just stick them in the ground, where they'll root and keep on growing.

Mazes cut in the lawn or stepping stones weaving a magical path through the borders (watch out for prickly plants) are instant winners, and any large weeping

IDEA 9, *Grass roots*, will help you fortify your lawn in preparation for the summer holidays.

Try another idea...

'I conducted a wide-ranging survey and asked my three children what they most wanted from a garden. The answers were immediate: tree house, tree house, mountain bike course,'
From *Gardening Mad* by MONTY DON

Defining idea...

trees a perfect hideaway. Trees also offer the chance for some kind of tree house but, if your carpentry skills aren't up to that, a rope tied to a sturdy branch is an instant escape route for many a fantastical game.

Talking of which, if there is somewhere on your plot that screams out secret den, then check it's safe – remove things like stinging nettles and rusty nails sticking out of fence posts – and let the kids call it their own. You can even lend them a helping hand to put up something a bit more permanent.

SAFETY FIRST

There are a few other health and safety issues but most are common sense. Clear up dog and cat mess, watch kids around water, don't let them eat soil, wash cuts ASAP (and check kids' tetanus jabs are up to date) and make sure tools are stored safely so your toddler isn't suddenly let loose wielding a vicious pronged fork.

If you've got kids the garden should be their domain as well as yours. Flourishing cover drives and wristy backhands should all be applauded not decried, and even off-target free kicks that decapitate delphiniums should be a cause for celebration – albeit through gritted teeth.

But children should also be viewed as willing helpers, with an attention span of at least half an hour, if you're lucky. So get them to do a worthwhile job such as picking up leaves, sorting out flower pots or even, under supervision, a spot of weeding or deadheading.

Keep it basic though, as asking a six year old to prune every third shoot back to the fifth bud is only going to end in tears. And it won't be theirs.

Q I've heard a lot about poisonous plants in the garden. Are the dangers real?

How did it go?

A *Among the most common poisonous garden plants are laburnum, with its seed pods that look like peas, monkshood (Aconitum) which causes a skin rash and is extremely poisonous if eaten, and the foxglove (Digitalis purpurea) which can cause changes to the heartbeat. For more tips on child-proofing your garden, visit the Royal Society for the Prevention of Accidents (RoSPA) website at www.rospa.co.uk.*

Q What about tempting their nostrils too?

A *There's a whole range of plants that smell of chocolate including Chocolate cosmos (Cosmos atrosanguineus), while the climber Akebia quinata, with its purpley-red flowers, smells of vanilla. The curry plant (Helichrysum italicum) has curry scented leaves which give off a spicy aroma on a warm, sunny day and, who knows, a hint of lavender may calm them down when things get overexcited.*

131

30

Winter wonderland

**Evergreens, dried seed-heads, berries and coloured stems
are the secret to year-round interest.**

A garden with winter interest makes
work for idle hands and gives you the
chance to enjoy those plants that actually look
at their best on a cold and frosty morning.

SHAPE AND STRUCTURE

Winter lays the structure of a garden bare. But if you plant evergreens for interest, and train and clip trees to give shape, your garden need never loose its sense of form. Even the hard landscaping provided by paths, steps, paving and walls helps to keep the garden together, while a well-chosen trellis, support or arch can provide a new, seasonal focal point.

If you're not an over-tidy gardener, then leave border plants with unusual seed-heads – such as *Phlomis*, *Sedum* and *Echinops* – well alone and enjoy their frosted shapes. Similarly, soft brown grasses can look warm and mellow in the winter light. If you do go for this approach, everything will need cutting back in February, before the new growth appears.

Here's an idea for you...

Bare, needle-less Christmas trees dumped outside back gates, in the vain hope that the bin men will show mercy, are a sure sign the festive season is over. Much better, though, to recycle them, either to be shredded at the local tip or cut up, with the biggest branches used to protect tender plants such as *Osteospermum* and the crowns of a young *Gunnera*. Alternatively, you could recycle the tree by planting it back in the garden. A yew tree can be carefully dug up and planted again each year, and with a bit of root pruning should last ten years or more. Keep it in moist compost whilst indoors and when replanting make sure the planting hole – which can be the same each year – is well drained, and add a good helping of manure. Yew is, of course, poisonous but unlikely to tempt the kids.

The coloured stems of the dogwood (*Cornus*) range from bright green and yellow through to scarlet, wine red and almost black. They're a must for winter colour, while the vivid, violet berries of *Callicarpa bodinieri* look positively tropical, and last well into December.

It's staggering how many small flowers can survive the winter weather. Appearing in early January, the delicate snowdrops (*Galanthus*) reliably force their heads through the cold, hard ground and go well with aconites and hellebores. For the best chance of getting snowdrops to take, and then colonise, buy them after they've finished flowering, when they're still 'green', and plant them where they won't dry out in summer.

Without the more blousy competition of the borders, evergreens come into their own at this time of year. A low boundary wall, a clipped ball or spiral of box (*Buxus*) or yew (*Taxus*), can look stunning, whilst slim conifers such as the Italian cypress (*Cupressus sempervirens*) provide upright accents at a time when most other plants have been cut down.

FROST AND SNOW

Glimpse a snow-covered garden and you're immediately whisked off to a land of make-believe, amid comments of 'it used to snow so much more when I were a lad'. It probably didn't, but enjoy it anyway.

A topping of snow along the box hedges reinforces their shape, while a sprinkle around the low-growing black grass (*Ophiopogon planiscapus* 'Nigrescens') shows off its striking foliage. But if there's a heavy covering keep an eye on upright growing conifers, and shake off the snow before it bends or snaps the branches.

A delicate covering of frost is also to be enjoyed, as long as you've taken all the right precautions to protect your tender plants and pots. Those that need their centres guarding against the cold, such as the tree fern and cordyline, should be wrapped up with straw, surrounded by chicken wire. Pots of half-hardy plants should be taken into a frost-free, sheltered place, or covered in bubble wrap or hessian, and raised off the ground.

Other anti-frost measures include insulating the outdoor tap, placing footballs in the pond to prevent it freezing over, and feeding the birds. Add in a bit of digging, turning the compost heap, running repairs to fences and walls, and cleaning your tools, and you might just have time to look at that seed catalogue before the first daffodil appears.

IDEA 20, *Shrubs*, gives details of the many and varied shrubs with winter interest.

Try another idea...

'**The flowers of late winter and early spring occupy places in our hearts well out of proportion to their size.**'
Gardening writer GERTRUDE S. WISTER

Defining idea...

How did it go?

Q You mention placing orders from seed catalogues but do I have to wait for spring before I start sowing?

A *Winter is a good time to get certain plants under way (if you have a heated propagator all the better). For bedding, sow pelargoniums and begonias at this time, while on the veg front start off broad beans, beetroot and peas in pots. You can also take root cuttings from* Acanthus, Echinops *and perennial poppies (*Papaver*).*

Q Can I plant shrubs and trees in winter or should I wait for spring?

A *Planting shrubs and trees when they're dormant is a good idea. Just make sure the ground isn't waterlogged, and frost isn't forecast.*

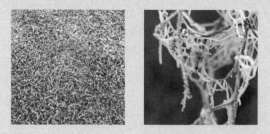

31

The sweet smell of success

Sit back in a deck chair surrounded by the heady fragrance of a well-positioned honeysuckle, or the calming scent of lavender, and suddenly all the hard work seems worthwhile.

Nature introduced scent to attract pollinating insects but it can also have a remarkable affect on Homo sapiens. Scent is evocative: smell hyacinths and you think of spring; sweet peas mingled with the aroma of freshly cut grass and summer holidays come flooding back; while bonfires and fallen leaves mean that autumn's approaching.

Fortunately, most types of plants come in scented forms from shrubs to climbers, perennials to annuals. But it's not just a question of choosing the right ones – you also need to place them where they will be truly appreciated.

Here's an idea for you...

It's a natural reaction to press your nose into a flower and take in its scent. Sometimes, though, you'll be disappointed and plants previously renowned for their perfume are now scentless, their smell bred out of them in favour of other features. So always check the label for a mention of fragrance if you are unable to sniff the flower itself. Sweet pea *odoratus* 'fragrantissima' is a dead give-away.

UNDERNEATH THE ARCHES

Arches, pergolas, even the porch are all crying out to be smothered in aromatic blooms. Honeysuckle is a traditional choice. The deciduous type (*Lonicera periclymenum*) is slightly less rampant than the evergreen version *L. japonica* 'Halliana' but both have delicious scent.

The romantics, of course, will choose roses, particularly climbers like the pink R. 'Mme Grégoire Staechelin', R. 'New Dawn' or R. 'Zéphirine Drouhin' (the latter is good for a north-facing aspect). You can prolong their interest too by combining them with a contrasting coloured clematis – sadly not fragrant – while the species rose R. *englanteria* will cover a fence with aromatic foliage and fill the air with the smell of fresh apples.

Defining idea...

'Another hint of it as the summer breeze stirs, and I know that the place I should be off to is my childhood.'
MICHAEL FRAYN writing about the scent of humble privet in *Spies*

More vigorous are the ramblers such as *Rosa filipes* 'Kiftsgate' or R. 'Rambling Rector', which have one splendid flush of thousands of small, white-scented flowers, but they do need space and some ruthless pruning every three years.

And you can bring some of that scent indoors too, by using rose petals to make pot-pourri, or as environmentally friendly, biodegradable confetti at a summer wedding.

Freesias are less commonly grown but *F*. 'Yellow River' and *F. alba*, in particular, have good perfume. They grow from half-hardy corms, flowering late winter to early spring, if given a sheltered site. Dig up after flowering and dry them off ready to replant in the autumn.

IDEA 26, *Cutting a dash*, will give you ideas on cutting scented flowers for the house and IDEA 42, *The herb garden*, tells you how to grow these culinary companions.

Try another idea…

Another unusual plant worth growing for its scent, shape and pale yellow flowers is the tree lupin (*Lupinus arboreus*). Don't panic – it's only a 1.5m shrub and will not get out of bounds as, sadly, it is short-lived. Also include for scent, if your garden is not too cold, the deep purple-pink *Daphne mesereum* or the paler *D. odora*. Remember too, the sunnier the position the greater the scent.

SCENT AND SEATS

A wisteria wrapped round a garden shed, or hovering over the compost heap, smacks of bad planning. Its subtle clove-like scent will be wasted. Scented plants need to be close at hand – you need to be able to smell them as you take in the early spring sunshine. So, either move a seat near to them or, if that's not practical, plant up the area around a fixed seat with those fragrant plants that will wow your senses, like pots of lilies – the most fragrant are *Lilium candidum* (Madonna Lily) or *L. regale.*

Many plants release their scent in the evenings, when the fading light means they have to try harder to attract insects. So if you've got a particular part of the garden for alfresco suppers, make sure the likes of the tall tobacco plant (*Nicotiana sylvestris*), evening primrose (*Oenothera*) and night scented stocks (*Matthiola bicornis*) are within nostril range.

'It is a golden maxim to cultivate the garden for the nose, and the eyes will take care of themselves.'
ROBERT LOUIS STEVENSON

Defining idea…

For centuries lavender has been used in perfumes, bath oils and sewn into bags. Inter-planted with pinks (*Dianthus*) and you'll have a winning combination of colour and scent. Both like well-drained soil and a sunny site.

Cat mint (*Nepeta*) provides an alternative scented edging, and don't forget the sweet peas, which should be placed where you regularly pass by or need to stop, say en route to the vegetable patch.

How did it go?

Q   Are there any winter shrubs with scent?

A   Surprisingly many shrubs provide scent in winter and at the beginning of spring. Chimonanthus praecox is not called 'Winter sweet' for nothing and the perfume of Hamamelis mollis is a real delight. (If your soil is chalky grow its lookalike, Cornus mas instead.) Mahonia is well worth growing for its dramatic evergreen foliage and delicately scented pale yellow flowers that bloom as winter passes.

Q   Are there some plants to avoid for their nasty smell?

A   Hawthorn blossom and the wild gelder rose have a foul smell when picked. Others, such as lilies and Viburnum badnantense, have a strong heady scent, which is lovely in the open air but too strong for some, in a confined space. The skunk cabbage (Lysichiten americanus) is an attractive bog plant with striking yellow flowers which, up close, smells (not unsurprisingly) of rotting cabbage.

32

Alright mate

If you think the idea of plants ganging up on insects is more suited to a sci-fi plot than a vegetable plot, then you've not heard of companion planting.

Companion planting is one of those ideas that's so simple and so obvious that it should be made compulsory in every garden. It's the organic way of keeping pests at bay and, while it has its critics, organic gardeners know it works.

And now they can back up this optimism with scientific fact, because boffins at a British university have proved that the marigold, a companion plant par excellence, really does contain an oil that repels aphids. The oil is released as a vapour which wafts around and deters bugs from landing on neighbouring plants.

BUZZ OFF

There are several different ways in which plants help each other. Many destructive insects locate their food by smell, so by interplanting possible targets with other plants that have a strong scent, you can confuse the enemy.

Here's an idea for you... **Buy a book on bugs, or borrow one from your local library. The vast majority of insects are actually beneficial to the garden, so it pays to learn what they look like before you inadvertently squash a friend not a foe.**

A second way is that some plants, through scent, colour and pollen, attract predatory insects into the garden. These predators will then seek and destroy the harmful insects which were about to have a good chew on your plants. And a third group virtually sacrifice themselves for the cause, luring the bad bugs away from the more valuable crops, to have a go at them instead.

So which plants are pally with which?

Well, whichever way you look at it, companion planting is not good news for the humble aphid. Garlic underneath roses is one way to keep greenfly at bay, but if any do get through, a sprig or two of dill nearby will attract wasps and hoverflies to hoover up the stragglers.

Aphids also turn their proboscis up at chervil, which is good interplanted with lettuce, and they don't care much for coriander either.

Yarrow (*Achillea millefolium*) is a fine flowering plant for the veg patch and another one that draws in the predators, including ladybirds, who love nothing better than an aphid picnic.

Try another idea... **For tips on getting the best from the veg plot try IDEA 15 *Small but perfectly formed*, and for more advantages of organic gardening see IDEA 34 *The good life*.**

One of the best vegetable combos is carrots and leeks, because while the latter repels carrot fly, the former gives off a smell offensive to the onion fly and leek moth (yes, apparently there is such a thing).

Another good double act sees tomatoes, with a bit of basil, deterring the asparagus beetles, while chemicals in the asparagus itself help prevent a harmful nematode attacking the roots of the tomato plant. Tomatoes are also one of the main beneficiaries of being mixed up with French marigolds

As you can see, this is all good stuff.

FRIENDS REUNITED

The trusty old nasturtium also has several uses. As well as a strong smell that keeps some aphids off the likes of broccoli and marrows, black fly love it but, being tough as old boots, it will rejuvenate after an attack, while other crops grow on unmolested.

Radishes can also be used as decoy, luring the likes of cucumber and flea beetles from their lunch of choice.

Of course you can help yourself by avoiding monoculture. If you offer up row after row of the same plant, with nothing planted between them, it's only a matter of time before the right pest flies past and tucks in. And, by growing aromatic plants that attract insects, you can give a helping hand to those plants that rely on good pollination to succeed.

'French marigolds are one of the best companion plants but they're of no culinary use whatsoever. Pot marigolds are not quite so good a companion but the petals are marvellous in soups and stews. Nasturtiums attract cabbage butterflies, so keeps them off the cabbages, and every bit of the nasturtium is edible. The flowers are wonderful in salads, and the seeds excellent pickled.
'But the best companion plant of all is the edible garland chrysanthemum, also called Shingiku in Japan and Choy Suy Green in Chinatown. It is particularly good with brassicas, keeping a lot of pests away, and attracting pollinators. You can use the young foliage in stir-fries, and the petals in salads. You can even use it as a cut flower. It couldn't be a better plant!'
BOB FLOWERDEW

Defining idea...

143

But companion planting isn't just about warding off insects. Plants can provide support for each other, act as windbreaks, create shade and act as ground cover – destroying weeds that would otherwise be fighting for valuable nutrients.

Yes, there's certainly an element of trial and error to companion planting. There are plenty of possible combinations and a few cases where the chemicals in one plant can actually inhibit the growth of another (see below). So it pays to keep a gardening diary to note down the combinations that work, and those that don't.

How did it go?

Q   **What's all this I've heard about nitrogen fixers?**

A   *Now this is a really clever form of companion planting. The fixers are leguminous plants like peas and beans, as well as lupins, although a clump of these on the veg patch would probably only attract an army of ravenous slugs. A bacteria in their roots converts nitrogen into a form that can be more easily absorbed by other plants. When the legume dies down, some of this nitrogen is left in the soil as a free feast for nitrogen-hungry plants like sweet corn, spinach and the brassicas.*

Q   **So are there any planting combinations that should be avoided?**

A   *Apparently fennel is blackballed by most other plants – so if you do grow it, keep it in solitary confinement. Carrots are no fan of dill either, while beans and peas detest the company of onions.*

33

From cabbages to kings

You've grown the basics, mastered the intricacies of crop rotation and shocked family and friends with your ability to put new potatoes on the table at Christmas. Well, now for something completely different.

We all love the challenge of growing something different, something new, something a bit unusual. Well it's not just flowers that throw up the odd horticultural challenge, the world of vegetables also has its own fair share of tricky customers.

But the effort involved in growing them is often rewarded when you serve them up for dinner. So, with salted butter at the ready, welcome to the molly-coddled, pampered world of asparagus and artichokes.

ASPARAGUS

Asparagus is a king among vegetables. It's a delicacy, and nothing else tastes quite like a freshly cut spear. And that is the key, because asparagus is a truly seasonal vegetable that should really only be eaten fresh in May and June, not shrink-wrapped for December. It's something that should be looked forward to, not devoured all year round.

Here's an idea for you... **Jerusalem artichokes are a perennial at the other end of the 'difficult to grow' spectrum. A member of the sunflower family, with attractive yellow flowers, they will grow just about anywhere, as long as it doesn't get water-logged. Simply plant the mature tubers in the spring and dig up the edible knobbly new ones as and when you want them, from autumn onwards. A nutty taste great for salads or boiled as a potato.**

The best way to grow asparagus is by using one-year-old crowns planted out in March or April. Only male plants produce spears, and all-male varieties give a higher yield, such as Franklim F1 or Lucullus F1. And remember it's the newly emerging spears that you eat, not the stalks that follow on.

If you're lucky, and garden on sandy, well-drained soil, the crowns can be planted directly into the ground. If not, you need to prepare an asparagus bed. Now this certainly isn't easy but you are planting something that will keep on cropping for about 20 years. And, once established, asparagus only needs basic care to keep going.

How big an area you devote to asparagus depends on the size of your garden but bear in mind the plants need to be around 30cm apart. And, although it likes an open site, asparagus isn't fond of strong winds. The bed needs to be well dug, well manured and free of perennial weeds. To improve your drainage, add a liberal amount of horticultural grit.

Next dig a trench about 30cm wide and 20cm deep and build up a ridge, about 8cm high, along the bottom. The crowns need to be handled very carefully and kept moist. Lay them over the top of the ridge, with the roots hanging down over the side, and cover with another 8cm of soil. Water well and then, in autumn, top up the trench to soil level. Now the waiting starts.

It pays to give the plants two years to get established, cutting the fronds down in November when they begin to yellow. Then in May of the third year you can begin to harvest. When the spears are 10–12cm high, cut them about 8cm below the soil, but stop by the end of the month and let the spears develop into the feathery fronds that will feed next year's growth.

Check out IDEA 32, *Alright mate*, for details about companion planting, while IDEA 42, *The herb garden*, will tell you how to grow some herbs to accompany your veg.

Try another idea...

For subsequent years, June 21 is traditionally the last date of the season.

ARTICHOKES

This is a great plant, albeit one that's a little mixed up. Globe artichokes are perennials that can grow up to 1.5m, so don't hide them away on the veg patch, because as well as bearing a delicious crop, they're great architectural plants for the back of the border too, where they'll also get the shelter and fertile soil they need.

'You grow it [asparagus] because it gives you a supply of absolutely fresh spears, but also to spit in the eye of the seasonless "food" industry and its joyless inducements of year-round treats.'
MONTY DON

Defining idea...

They're also a bit on the fussy side, which is why there's a challenge in growing them. They're best grown from root offsets, or rooted suckers (success with seeds is far more variable). These you can buy first time round, but for successive years take cuttings from your own plants.

The soil needs to be well-drained and the offsets, which should be about 20cm long with their leaves still attached, should be planted 1m apart and about 5cm deep.

They need protection from full sun in the early stages and should be mulched and watered once they've become established.

Like asparagus, this is another plant that requires patience, and in the first year you should remove the edible flower heads to encourage more growth.

Cropping really begins in the year after planting. Allow around six stems to develop and then harvest the kinghead, the bud at the top of the leading stem, when it's still green and tightly folded. Leave it too long and it will open into a large purple thistle-like flower – very pretty but not very edible.

Leave about 5cm of the stem attached, and harvest all the secondary heads in June and July. They will carry on producing for up to five years, but as soon as they die down in autumn give them a good mulch and protect the crown from frost.

How did it go?

Q   How come my asparagus just never got going?

A   *Lots of possibilities here but one of the most common problems is overzealous weeding. Asparagus has shallow roots that can easily be damaged by clumsy hoeing. And you really must stick to the harvesting regime if your asparagus is ever going to flourish.*

Q   You've tempted me. Is there another tricky veg I can grow?

A   *Cauliflowers present a real challenge and are fussy in the extreme, needing plenty of space and water. But there are some amazing new and tasty varieties such as 'Graffiti' with its purple florettes and the spiky lime green version, romanesco 'Celio'.*

34

The good life

Gardening organically is as much about common sense as it is about being chemical free.

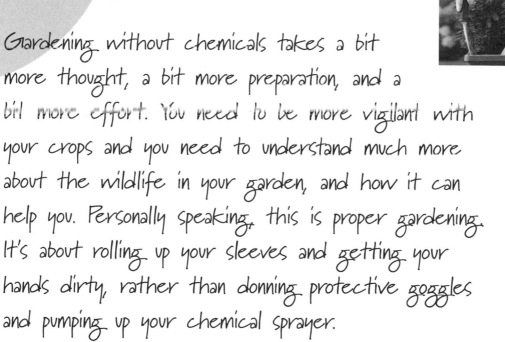

Gardening without chemicals takes a bit more thought, a bit more preparation, and a bit more effort. You need to be more vigilant with your crops and you need to understand much more about the wildlife in your garden, and how it can help you. Personally speaking, this is proper gardening. It's about rolling up your sleeves and getting your hands dirty, rather than donning protective goggles and pumping up your chemical sprayer.

DIRTY BUSINESS

Soil and its structure are at the heart of organic gardening. Get that right, so the logic goes, and strong, healthy plants will follow. And the best way to improve your soil is by feeding it with organic matter, which encourages the creatures living in it to do their bit, and will improve its structure and fertility.

Here's an idea for you... **Fed up with trying to coax some life into your lawn? Then why not turn all or part of it into a wild flower meadow. You'll only need to cut it a few times a year, and the wildlife will love it so much more than a close-cut turf. But remember, wild flowers like nutrient-poor soil, so it pays to skim off the top 15cm of topsoil before you start planting.**

By using your own compost heap, you are effectively digging back in what grew in your borders the previous year, returning all those nutrients from whence they came.

With the soil improved, the rest is common sense. Buy disease-resistant plants where possible, make sure the pH of the soil is to their liking, and that the spot you've chosen suits their needs.

It's not just your use of insecticides and herbicides that you need to reconsider, but fertilisers too. Remember you're growing for the pot or the vase, not the show table, so do your plants really need all that feed? And there's plenty of evidence to suggest overfed plants are a lot more attractive to pests.

If you do carry on feeding, think about the organic alternatives such as bonemeal for adding phosphate, or dried blood for a quick fix of nitrogen. Liquid fertilizers made from comfrey or animal manures are also useful, especially for container-grown plants.

But gardening organically is about much more than avoiding pesticides and creating your own compost. It's a much broader concept that takes in issues such as conserving natural resources, avoiding pollution, and recycling.

Take peat for example. It makes our blood boil that so many gardeners and garden centres continue to use it. Peat is a finite resource and, to be quite honest, it's virtually knackered already. Peat bogs are some of our richest and most diverse natural habitats, yet in the UK alone a staggering 2.55 million cubic metres is dug up for horticultural use each year.

There's much more on making sure you grow the right plants in the right soil in IDEA 1, *Did the earth move?*

Try another idea...

Yet some professional gardeners still swear by it, saying that it remains by far the best medium for growing a wide range of plants. And that may well be true, but the alternatives are improving all the time and where's the logic in destroying a natural habitat in order to create an artificial one?

Trials suggest that peat-free alternatives aren't as effective as the real thing, but that isn't really the point. This is a fantastic opportunity to experiment with your own mixes, using an alternative such as coir, bark chippings or a peat-free multi-purpose compost as your base. Then simply add your own measure of top soil, garden compost, sand and grit, and see what works with your seedlings, plants you've re-potted or your longer-term containers. OK, it may take a few seasons to get it right, but what's the hurry?

Recycling is also a key part of gardening organically, from making your own compost with kitchen waste to buying trugs and weeding buckets made from recycled car tyres. It's also about recycling water by using water butts; using prunings as plant supports; collecting and sharing your own seeds (but leave some for the birds!); even buying a kit to make your own biodegradable plant pots from newspaper.

'The chemical gardener goes to war on a daily basis and perceives his garden akin to a "battlezone", whereas the "organic" gardener tends to diffuse potential problems before they have the opportunity to escalate.'
PATRICK VICKERY, Gardening writer and nursery owner.

Defining idea...

Then there are all those things which are really just good gardening practice, such as rotating your crops, encouraging beneficial insects into the garden, and providing habitats and food sources for friendly predators.

Gardening organically is far from a panacea to all our gardening ills. You will still take losses (perhaps more at first), still have to face up to failures and still get frustrated as slugs engulf your delphiniums. But to most of us gardening is a hobby, a pastime, a challenge. And meeting this challenge by working with nature, not against her, is so much more rewarding than reaching for the bug buster.

 How did it go?

Q   I've heard a lot about no-digging gardens. Is it organic?

A   Undisturbed soil is a much better place for many beneficial bugs and organisms, and a policy of no-digging can also preserve soil structure and cut back on moisture loss. But it's only an option where the soil structure is already good and if you've got the time to really keep on top of the weeds.
   On the other hand, digging is the only way of incorporating bulky stuff into the soil – worms can only help so much! Breaking up the soil can also improve drainage, aerate it and improve root penetration. It also destroys weeds and exposes pests in the soil to winter weather and predators.

Q   Am I OK using John Innes compost?

A   While there is a peat-free version, John Innes composts do still contain peat, albeit a small amount. And by the way, John Innes is a type of compost based on loam rather than a brand, and was developed by Mr Innes in the late nineteenth century. So now you know.

35

Wildlife friendly

With intensive farming and the countryside fast disappearing under concrete and brick, our gardens have become a vital green oasis to many birds, insects and animals.

A garden without wildlife is a pretty sorry site. No bird song, no pollinating insects, no frogs or toads lurking behind the garden shed. No fun.

On a purely practical level, of course, by attracting hoverflies, tits and hedgehogs into the garden we're employing our own free, organic band of pest controllers.

But to become wildlife friendly doesn't mean you need to replant your garden from scratch, let it become an overgrown mess, or stop growing the plants you love. You just need to make a few adjustments, and employ some other organic methods of gardening at the same time. After all, it would be pretty pointless attracting song thrushes into the garden to help keep snails under control, while at the same time continuing to use slug pellets which could poison the birds.

There are four basics you need to provide to attract wildlife: food, water, shelter and somewhere to breed. But once they know these essentials for survival are all

Here's an idea for you...

To a toad, a drain is a des res. They love them, so hold off using bleach when you give them a clean. Instead, use one of the new 'green' bactericides that use naturally occurring bacteria rather than chemicals, and are harmless to wildlife.

available in your garden, they'll come back time and time again.

So here are some suggestions on how to get the bees buzzing and the birds singing on your plot.

IT'S A FOOD THING

Try and find room in the garden for plants that wildlife enjoy, such as the seed-heavy teasels, sunflowers and thistles, or the berry-laden cotoneasters and hollies. They look great and birds will love them.

Grow plants that are rich in pollen and nectar too, such as *Verbena bonariensis*, buddleia, sedums, eupatorium and nepeta. As well as pollinators, these will also attract predatory insects into the garden, such as ladybirds and lacewings, which will lay their eggs on the plants. In due course these will hatch into larvae, which are the aphid-eating machines of the insect world.

In order to encourage maximum diversity, try and combine elements of a woodland area, wild flower meadow and a pond or boggy area in your garden.

The simplest of water features can make a difference – even an old washing bowl sunk into the ground in a quiet corner of the garden, part-filled with stones, will attract frogs and toads. And you can give nature a helping hand by asking friends with ponds both for a jar of bug-rich pond water, and any spare frog spawn they've got lying about. Bird baths are also important, both as a source of fresh drinking water and as somewhere to bathe.

GIMME SHELTER

Try to find an area of the garden you can let grow wild, where plants like stinging nettles can flourish. This 'weed' plays an important part in the life cycle of over 100 different species of insect, including several butterflies.

A great way of achieving winter interest in the garden is to resist the urge to cut everything back and tidy up in the autumn. Granted, some jobs need to be done but dead and decaying plants add an air of mystery to any border, as well as providing refuge for overwintering insects.

The likes of beech, blackthorn, hazel, hornbeam and hawthorn are excellent trees when it comes to offering wildlife shelter. And log piles are hotels with 24-hour room service to many bugs, hedgehogs and grass snakes. The insects and fungi that gradually eat the wood will, in turn, feed other creatures in the garden.

There's a whole range of purpose-built shelters too – from lacewing chambers to ladybird towers, nester kits for pollinating bees to butterfly houses. And the hedgehog house nestled under a forsythia in the front garden will certainly raise a few eyebrows.

IDEA 28, *On the waterfront*, shows you how to attract some water-loving wildlife to your garden with your own pond.

Try another idea...

'**Wildlife gardens have already saved the frog, the toad and the newt. Our bird population is enhanced dramatically by service station wildlife gardens which provide a lifeline every winter. Your garden, however small it is, can make a real difference.**'
From *How to make a Wildlife Garden* by CHRIS BAINES

Defining idea...

Garden birds, particularly nesting ones, devour caterpillars, leatherjackets and chafer grubs, as well as slugs and snails. So a few well-sited nesting boxes, out of the reach of your pet moggy, will work wonders.

This is just a taster of the simple changes you can make to ensure that local wildlife thrives and that your garden is with nature rather than against it.

How did it go?

Q **I've done all you said but still can't attract any animals into the garden. What am I doing wrong?**

A *It may sound obvious, but have you left them a way in? Birds and insects can fly in but most gardens are pretty much sealed off from the outside world at ground level, with brick walls, fences and gravel boards preventing hedgehogs and frogs from getting to the tasty treat you've so thoughtfully left out. Then again, do you have a cat or dog that is chasing the wildlife away?*

Q **If I keep putting food out for the birds, will it put them off their main meal, i.e. the pests on my plants?**

A *True to some extent. It probably pays to lay off refilling the bird table at the height of the summer, to encourage the tits and robins to forage in the border for their grub. If you do put nuts out for the birds during the summer, remember to put them in a mesh container so that the parents don't feed their chicks with chunks that are too big, and potentially lethal.*

36

Let there be light

From 500-watt security lights to a dozen or so strategically placed tealights on the decking, lighting your garden can be an illuminating business.

So why bother to light your garden? Well, it's a cliché but true, all the same — many of us now see the garden as an extra room, an extra living space that we want to use and enjoy. So it stands to reason that we want to spend as much time in it as possible. Even when the moon's out.

There's a number of different ways you can go about lighting your garden and most of them you should be able to complete with only minimal (although vital) professional help.

Of course you could call in the professionals to do the lot. Mains-powered units are certainly impressive but installing them means a lot of upheaval and mess, as the

Here's an idea for you...

Whatever you do, don't dismiss the humble outdoor fairy light. They look great wrapped round the trunk of a tree or draped over a trellis, especially during the festive season. Ropes of lights are also effective, just twisting through your borders or lighting up the outline of a garden structure.

armoured cables need to be buried at least 60cm under your borders. There's the cost as well, and don't forget the impact it will have on the electricity bill.

Solar lights are a good choice and relatively cheap to buy. They're also a solution if you haven't got an electricity source for the garden, and useful too at the end of a long garden, where cables won't reach anyway.

Mounted on spikes, solar lights can be easily moved around the garden (best to site them in a sunny spot!) and, whilst they're not powerful enough to light up individual plants and walls, they're great used for lining paths or showing where steps are. For special occasions, flares look fantastic dotted amongst the beds – the citronella ones will also help keep the midges at bay – and lanterns with simple tealights are also effective.

But for a more permanent arrangement that can highlight the best aspects of your garden, go for a simple off-the-shelf number from the local DIY store. There are a number of kits where you just run the cable round the garden, clipping the lights on wherever takes your fancy. How many you'll need obviously depends on the size of your garden.

As for power, a 12- or 24-volt system uses a transformer plugged into the mains to reduce the voltage. Then plug the lights into the transformer. If you need an outside waterproof plug, this is where the electrician comes in.

So how to use them?

Spotlighting is used to highlight particular plants or garden features. It creates dramatic effects, drawing the eye towards it, and so works well when seen from a distance.

Up lighting involves placing the light below the plant, angling it so that it shines up through the branches or foliage. It's particularly effective used to light a tree or large shrub, and is a good way of adding a bit of extra height to a garden. Remember, you don't have to stick to white light. Create different moods with blues, purples or flame shades.

The reverse is down lighting, which is the best way to create pools of light. Fix the spotlights to a fence, pergola or tree, or on the wall around a patio or decking. They can then be used to pick out certain features, such as a garden ornament, or particular pots and containers.

The term 'grazing' refers to lights that are angled to show off a particular surface, such as a dry-stone wall, or the slats of a fence. It's also a clever way to bring out the colour on a painted wall.

You can use a hidden light source to silhouette plants or objects from behind, creating intriguing shadows and giving the garden depth. It's particularly good with architectural plants, such as yuccas and phormiums.

To find out how to build some of the structures you may wish to light up, see IDEA 40, Structurally sound.

Try another idea...

'Filling anything other than your own private space with any kind of light is an intrusion and invasion of privacy. Garden lights must be personal and intimate. The light they throw must rest modestly within the shadows they create.'
MONTY DON

Defining idea...

159

Waterproof lights in ponds or fountains are dramatic but can verge on the tacky unless carefully positioned. Use them to pick out moving water, rather than flooding the whole pool with light. There's also a range of solar-powered globes that float on water.

However, all this is not to say that darkness doesn't have a beauty all of its own, or that your neighbours want their lawn lit up by a badly positioned spot. There needs to be a touch of subtlety about any lighting scheme you install. In most towns and cities it's already impossible to escape the orange glow of a thousand street lights, but it's phosphorescence we really don't want to add to. So with gardens lights, less is certainly more.

How did it go?

Q   I've never been happy using electricity in the garden. Any other safety tips you can pass on?

A   *If you're running cables up and down the garden, whether for lights or power tools, always use a residual current device (RCD). This circuit breaker will shut down the power should you inadvertently cut through the cable.*

Q   Will lighting up my garden put off the wildlife?

A   *Not necessarily so. A gentle white light fixed on the corner of your house will enable you to watch hedgehogs, foxes or badgers at night, if they frequent your garden in search of food. Turn your inside lights off for a better effect.*

37

The can-can

All plants need water to survive, but how can we maximise its effect in the garden, while minimising waste?

Water is fast becoming one of our most precious natural resources, which is why, as gardeners, we need to use it as effectively and as sparingly as everyone else.

There are some basic rules that are well worth sticking to, in particular collecting it where you can. Don't just 'splash it all over' either, as this is one area where 'little and often' is the wrong maxim. A long and thorough soak is much better that a gentle sprinkle – once a week rather, than once a day.

WATER COURSE

For starters, only water when your plants need it and in summer never water during the day as it will have no lasting benefit and most of the water will simply evaporate. Best wait until the evening, so the water can do its bit overnight. With hosepipe in hand, it's a great way to relax after a hot day, and enjoy the garden.

Here's an idea for you...

To cope with the heavy demands of newly planted shrubs and trees, sink a piece of plastic pipe down to the roots after planting. Leave the top just above ground level. Angle the pipe towards the roots and you can water them directly. This has the added advantage of encouraging roots to grow downwards rather than upwards towards surface water. In between waterings, place a stone or cork in the opening to prevent mice or pests crawling in and feasting on your new investment.

Having got the timing right, how's your aim? Try and get the water straight to the plant's roots. A garden sprinkler pointing up in the air will refresh the leaves but unless left on for hours, its spray will never reach the soil. Use a hosepipe on low pressure instead and aim it on the roots. Count to a hundred (two hundred if you can bear it) for each shrub or climbing plant, especially those having to compete for moisture, say under a tree or against a wall. Mature shrubs and trees should cope with dry conditions in most summers.

Making your soil as spongy as possible will help retain the moisture, and you can do this by adding well-rotted compost in autumn or spring each year.

The final rule is to keep the soil cool. Covering it entirely with plants will help retain moisture and minimise evaporation.

The common garden hose is now quite a sophisticated beast with controllable flow, adjustable sprays and recoiling versions that can even wind themselves up after use. But consider all your options before simply leaving them on for long periods. In particularly dry areas a seep hose may be more economical, letting out water drip by drip and keeping the ground constantly moist below the surface. Connected to a timing switch these secret soakers can also be set to water at night.

But for the butts a lot of water would be lost down the drain. There's a sense of satisfaction in getting something for free, and collecting rainwater comes under this category. It's also coming straight from the heavens, so is free from contamination. Place two or three together with connecting pipes and the bulk of your watering needs will be met. Use green plastic butts where they're out of sight and old cider or sherry barrels for show.

Don't forget the greenhouse too. Fix guttering to a butt on at least one side, and it will mean an end to all those long trips back and forwards to the outdoor tap, saving time and effort, as well as water.

You can also use this supply to keep a watering can topped up at 'room temperature'. Cold water will be too much of a shock for seedlings and young plants. Invest in a can that has a fine wire mesh attached to the rose which prevents the holes in the rose from becoming blocked up – usually the curse of fine spray cans.

IDEA 7, *Sweet smelling brown stuff*, will help you produce all-important moisture retaining compost, and IDEA 1, *Did the earth move?*, suggests some drought-tolerant plants.

Try another idea...

'Water – its supply and its quality – is as an essential issue in our new world as it is everywhere else'
TIM SMIT

Defining idea...

HOLIDAY INSURANCE

All gardeners deserve a break but asking the neighbours to do the watering is a tall order. At least make it simple for them by setting up a self-watering system using capillary matting (readily available at garden centres). Place it on some polythene and cut a strip to act as a wick, running from under the matting to a covered container, set at a lower level. Place thirsty plants on top of the matting and let them gently sip away. All your neighbours will have to do is keep the container topped up every four days or so. Remember to water well before you go and don't forget to bring back a bottle of something, other than water, as a thank you.

How did it go?

Q   You say to be sparing with water so which plants need it most?

A   *Vulnerable plants include those with shallow roots, seedlings, young plants or those newly planted, leafy veg (like spinach and runner beans) and fruiting trees or bushes. Shrubs that form flower buds at the end of summer– such as camellias – will need a good drink in summer, to swell the buds.*

Q   Can I also recycle used water from the house?

A   *Yes, you can re-use bath or washbasin water, but not if it's had detergent mixed in it.*

38

Dear diary

Why keeping a record of your garden, and what you do in it, makes sense.

A garden is in a permanent state of evolution; it's never finished. That's what makes it so interesting and all the more reason to keep a note of its changing and maturing face. And make a photographic record too, because like a fisherman's tale, last year's crops, herbaceous borders and annuals were always bigger, better and brighter. Or were they?

By taking notes we learn where we went wrong as well as what we did right, so influencing future decisions. There are a number of ways of doing this but, whether in a notepad or on a computer, in the form of a full-blown diary or random scribblings, your jottings will act as important reminders and tips for next year and beyond.

Here's an idea for you...

Draw up a tree chart of your garden. Trees are major investments and should be around a long time. Make a plan and note the type of tree, where it was purchased and when it was planted. The chart will be an interesting reference point and vital information should you need any tree surgery. You could also leave it for the next gardeners, should you decide to sell up and move on.

FORWARD PLANNING

So why take notes? There are some tasks you just don't want to miss where a diary note is crucial. Leave shearing off the old hellebore or epimedium leaves too late and you will run the risk of cutting off the new growth with the old. February is the time to do this – early for the hellebores and late for the epimediums. Also in February, make a note to trim hedges before birds start nesting.

The catalogues thudding on the mat will leave you in no doubt when to order things! But when your seed order arrives it's useful to log when you need to plant which variety. You don't want to find them forgotten on the shelf at the end of the year.

Make a diary entry to check tree ties twice a year in November and May, and to get the mower serviced in December, which is often the cheapest time. A memo at the end of November to clear the *Clematis montana* out of the guttering, as it makes a bid for the chimney stack, will ensure you remove all the dead leaves at the same time.

Defining idea...

'A garden is never so good as it will be next year.'
THOMAS COOPER
(US photographer/teacher)

If you look at the herbaceous border when it's in full flow the gaps and mistakes will be obvious – to you if not to others. You imagine you'll easily remember to move that leggy phlox, or divide up the crowded crocosmia, but you won't. Come the autumn, when all looks dead and brown, you'll be struggling to recognise the plants, let alone remember what you intended to do with them. So keep 'notes on the border' and, during the summer, jot down which plants to move, divide or keep for seed.

Idea 4, **Don't pay the nurseryman**, reminds you when to take which cuttings.

Try another idea…

A self-taught, enthusiastic and successful gardening friend was highly organised – too much so at times! But her 'order book' was worthy of publication. She recorded annually all the seeds, bulbs and plants she purchased – the supplier, the variety, quantity and price. This is a great way to avoid disappointment when you want to re-order and can't remember the name or the supplier.

Technology not only helps with lists and reminders but it simplifies keeping a photographic record of your garden too. A basic digital camera is an inexpensive way of recording the gardening year. The first snowdrop to appear, a planting combination that really worked, or the hosta, planted for its bold blue leaves, putting on an unexpected golden autumn show.

Some people are born list makers. Whether this is you or not, two lists are especially recommended. One for gardening items you would like to receive as presents – should anyone ask. The other, an immediate 'to do' list for the coming week or month. And, if it's not too daunting, start a 'major projects' list as well.

'The man around the corner keeps experimenting with new flowers every year, and now has quite an extensive list of things he can't grow.'
WILLIAM VAUGHAN, writing in the 16th Century

Defining idea…

How did it go?

Q   How can I keep an account of the names of my plants as well as my trees?

A   *It's difficult to keep plants labelled in the garden and fancy markers are expensive. So keep a written or computer list with a page for each section of the garden; fruit and veg patch, border, shrub bed, etc. List plants as you purchase them, with a description and position. This task alone will help you remember the names!*

Q   What can I use as a prompt to set up my first diary?

A   *Start reading and watching. TV gardening programmes, newspaper columns and magazines contain detailed 'action needed' sections, covering when to prune what, when to take cuttings and care for your lawn, together with timely reminders for your border, vegetables and fruit plots, under glass and in the pond. Find a writer or presenter who shares your gardening philosophy and stick with them.*

39

Your own little powerhouse part II

As well as bulbs and corms, there's a range of other bulbous plants that can bring life to your borders. Welcome to the world of tubers and rhizomes.

Many, although certainly not all, of this wide range of plants form part of that loose collection of bloomers, summer flowering bulbs. It's also a group that happens to contain some of our most popular and colourful plants, although only a few are hardy, so they'll need bringing in over winter.

A quick word on definitions for all the lexicographers out there. A tuber is a swollen underground stem base which, unlike a bulb, has roots growing from the sides as well as the bottom. There are also lots of growth points scattered over its upper surface, perhaps best seen on the most common tuber of them all, the humble spud. In the herbaceous border you're more likely to recognise the good old dahlia (although this is actually a tuberous root, but let's not split hairs!).

Here's an idea for you...

Let's face it, even to the trained eye, one end of a begonia looks much the same as the other. Obviously this is a problem when it comes to planting so, if you're not sure which is which, put the tuber in a plastic bag of damp compost or perlite for a couple of weeks. Shoots will form and you'll be able to plant them outside, the right way up.

An individual tuber can last for years, with some, like the cyclamen, getting bigger and bigger rather than producing offsets, while others, like the dahlia, are soon crying out to be divided.

Rhizomes are thickened underground stems that have chosen to grow horizontally rather than vertically. Roots grow directly from the underside and the main growing point is at one end, although there may be additional buds along its sides. Irises and cannas are good examples, although quite different in appearance.

TUBULAR SWELLS

Dahlias are among the easiest garden plants to grow, with a colour for everyone, and a range of different flower forms from the simple single to the blousy pompon. Plant in late spring with the eyes about 10cm below the surface. They thrive in well-drained, rich soil and need full sun to reach their maximum potential. They generally bloom from midsummer until the first frost but with so many varieties (around 20,000 at the last count), each responding to slightly different conditions, it pays to pick one or two you like the look of, and then read up on them.

Defining idea...

'No other flower sucks in light so voluptuously and returns it with such velvet intensity of pigment as an iris.'
MONTY DON

The tuberous begonia is the only one of the begonia family that you can treat as a perennial to be grown outdoors. Plant out (just below the surface as they're prone to rotting) in May, in well-drained soil with some shade. But make sure there's plenty of room between the plants – perhaps as much as 50–60cm – to allow the air to circulate, and give them space to grow.

IRIS EYES ARE SMILING

For full details on how to store dahlias over winter see IDEA 5, *Indian summer*, and for more on bulbs and corms see IDEA 14, *Your own little powerhouse part 1.*

Try another idea...

Irises, which grow from fleshy, creeping rhizomes, are divided into three groups: bearded, beardless and crested. Once again some further reading will be required as some like acid soils, others alkaline; some open position with their rhizomes partly exposed, others dappled shade. Bearded irises are the most common type, and have wonderfully extravagant blooms. There are cultivars ranging from a miniature dwarf such as *Iris pumila*, with its white, purple or yellow flowers, to the taller *I. florentina*, with its blue-tinged, white flowers, and vanities that will flower from early to late spring. The name comes from the short hairs on the back of the petals just in case you were wondering! These unshaven beauties must be planted in gritty, sandy soil, with their rhizomes exposed on the surface, where they can be baked by the sun.

If your garden has heavy, badly drained soil, you'd be wise to consider some of the beardless irises which, although not as colourful as their 'hirsute' cousins, will put up with more moist soil. The bright blue flowered *I. sibirica* does very well in damp ground. Plant this type, with their more slender rhizomes, below the surface and allow them to spread.

Defining idea...

'If you observe a really happy man you will find him building a boat, writing a symphony, educating his son, growing double dahlias in his garden, or looking for dinosaur eggs in the Gobi Desert.'
W. BERAN WOLFE (American psychiatrist)

171

With cannas, it's a good idea to start them off indoors, in a propagator if you've got one. Cover with just a centimetre or so of compost and water sparingly. Pot them on when the shoots are about 5cm high.

Alternatively, they can be planted directly into the garden in about mid-May. Whichever method you choose, give them a spot that's got rich, sandy loam soil, preferably in full sun. They also need regular watering.

Finally, a quick mention for one of our favourite plants, Solomon's seal (*Polygonatum*). This is a woodland plant with various varieties that do well in different conditions. All are hardy and rhizomatous, and most have strong architectural foliage with fantastic greenish-white drooping flowers. Superb.

How did it go?

Q   Can I take root cuttings from my tubers?

A   *No, it's best to divide tubers with a sharp knife once they've started to regrow in early spring. Always making sure each part has at least one good bud. You can, though, take soft cuttings from the new growth that appears in spring, to swell your stocks.*

Q   My irises are doing well – too well in fact. Should I divide them?

A   *Definitely. Plants like irises grow in clumps which can easily get congested. Regular dividing (every three years or so) can breathe new life into them, and that means better blooms. You also get more plants to spread around the garden. Simply dig up the whole clump just after flowering and cut off the new rhizomes from the old woody centre, which you can chuck on the compost heap.*

40

Structurally sound

The familiar sound of splintering wood, the gentle crash of bricks, the air turning blue as you strike thumb, not nail. Oh, the joys of DIY.

For some, the pleasure of building something with their own hands is a complete anathema. Why, they reason, when the local garden centre has gazebos and arches stacked to the ceiling, should you even think about dragging out a box of tools that hasn't seen the light of day since you were forced to 'customise' a flat-pack wardrobe several years previously?

For others, it's a challenge and a chance to see how much of those woodwork lessons at school really sunk in.

Timber, ideally hardwood, is likely to be your key garden material. Best bought from a timber merchant or sawmill, rather than a garden centre, you need to make

Here's an idea for you...

Do not dismiss out of hand using reconstituted stone or good old concrete. The advantage of these materials is that you can make things to the size and shape required – a concrete seat for instance. Make a wooden frame corresponding to the seat-top's dimensions and stand it on a plastic sheet, leaving any wrinkles or creases in place (these will give the seat an age-old look). Shovel in the concrete. When set, mortar the top on two similarly made pillars.

sure it's been treated or pressurized. This means it's been submerged in tanks with the preservative forced into the core of the timber.

Failing that, use an untreated hardwood. Beech is fairly common, relatively inexpensive and, if bought from a timber merchant, it should have been properly seasoned, although it will still need further protection from the elements. Apply at least two liberal coats of preservative. You won't need to re-apply it and you'll be rewarded with a structure that will fend off everything the weather can throw at it.

OK, that's the wood sorted, now you need to put it together. Whether you're contemplating a pergola, an arch, or rustic table, consider trying some basic joinery rather than slamming in nails to hold it together.

There is method in the madness because, while using nails is undeniably quicker, the vagaries of the weather and constant use will soon have your structure wobbling or even collapsing, as the nails loosen.

Much stronger is a simple cross-halving joint, which is also perfect for a standard pergola built from 10 × 10cm timber. (You can even inspect the construction method at any garden centre.) A piece is cut out of one strut to slot into another. The principal working tools you need are a tenon saw, broad chisel and a mallet. No need for glue.

The picture overleaf shows a bench and table made with round, treated beech posts and held together with cross-halving, some mortice and tenon joints, and a few screws. The rough timber means the joints aren't accurate to the millimetre but they've stood in all weathers for 15 years, and are as good as new.

There's more fancy brickwork in IDEA 46, *Up the garden path*, and tips on where to put them in IDEA 6, *Design without the despair*.

Try another idea...

If you're not a 'brickie' by trade it's probably safer for everyone that you confine any brickwork to say a retaining wall, or something nice and low!

Before you start, always make sure the bricks for your project match those of your house, lest you end up with an unsightly mishmash of a wall made of London stock running alongside a house built of multicoloured, handmade bricks. Less of an eyesore, but also important, is to match the bond or pattern of the house bricks.

Building a free-standing dry stone wall is an exceptional skill. And, if only for safety reasons, should be left to an expert. However, a low dry stone retaining wall is much easier, and the end result offers endless scope for growing aubrieta, alyssum, campanula, and many other rock-loving plants. Just two tips. Lay the first course at least partially buried to give the wall some stability and, as you build, lean the stones slightly into the material you are retaining.

'Most of us tend to be very timid in our selection of external features, with the result that they do not make a strong enough statement within the garden's design, or are swamped by plants.'
JOHN BROOKES, garden designer

Defining idea...

175

How did it go?

Q   What about using screws instead of nails?

A   *Screws can be used as additional support, but not as a replacement for a joint. Don't forget, screw into the cross grain not the end grain or they'll soon work loose. Once you've mastered the cross-halving joint, the basic pergola doesn't need screws or nails. What's more, if a strut is damaged it can easily be replaced without having to wrestle with screws or, worse still, rusty nails.*

Q   What can I do to save a stone wall ravaged by ivy?

A   *Pull away the ivy and remove the loose stones temporarily, if it helps you reach any ivy rooted in the wall. It's a good idea to burn the ivy but bear in mind it's highly flammable. You also need to remove all the loose mortar. There are products you can spray into the wall to kill off the ivy but new mortar and good pointing will also prevent re-growth. The ivy will start again outside the wall, so just cut it off wherever it raises its head.*

41

How to get the most from your containers

Even the biggest gardens have pots and containers brightening up a terrace, bringing life to a plain brick wall, or even lurking in the borders, adding a bit of timely, seasonal colour.

'Gardening with pots and containers — not like the real thing is it?' a friend quipped when we mentioned this chapter in the book. Oh, such folly! Containers are not an easy way out. They depend on you for constant food and water more than anything you have growing in the borders.

Yet this is also the beauty of containers – you're in control. You can move them, replant them, and keep them out of the reach of slugs and snails. You can let your imagination run wild, moving plants round as they come into bloom. And you can even surreptitiously place a few in your borders if they need a bit of a lift.

Here's an idea for you... **To speed up that aging process on your terracotta or stone pots, a liberal coating of natural yoghurt will give the mosses and lichens a helping hand. Make sure you've soaked the pots in water first and once 'painted' put them somewhere cool, damp and shady to let the bacteria do its work.**

GETTING KITTED OUT

Plants will grow in just about anything, from ceramic vases to old watering cans, wooden planters to your own 'mock' rock troughs. But, even in small gardens, bear in mind you'll always make more impact by using large containers.

Terracotta pots are the pot of choice for most people. They look natural, age beautifully and are heavy enough to stand up to blustery conditions. But they're also very porous and, unless you line them with something like a bin bag with a few drainage holes added, they will soak up water before the plants get a look in. And stopping this water leaching into the terracotta also means they're less likely to crack when it freezes (and that goes for the so-called frost-proof pots as well).

The first thing to check with any container is that it has drainage holes at the bottom – if it doesn't, get the drill out. Next add some crocks, stones or old bits of polystyrene from broken up seed trays, to stop those vital drainage holes clogging up. An old cloth over the crocks will filter the water and stop your compost washing away.

Now for the compost itself. Tempting as it may be, avoid using garden soil as you don't know what pests and disease could be lurking in it. Better to use a loam based compost such as John Innes No2, or a general potting or multipurpose compost – peat-free of course.

However, despite its impeccable green credentials, the downside of peat-free alternatives is that they dry out quicker than peat, so add a bit of leaf mould or garden compost, and some water-retentive crystals too.

For acid lovers like rhododendrons, you'll need to use lime-free ericaceous compost.

MIX AND MATCH

If you're planting up a container with several different varieties of plant, make sure that they all enjoy the same growing conditions. Arrange the plants, in their pots, on top of the compost first, imagining how they will fill out as they grow.

Start planting with the plant in the tallest pot (and therefore the biggest root ball) first. Put this in place and then add more compost to achieve the correct planting height for the smaller plants. This will also stop them sinking and ensure that their roots are in contact with the compost.

Always try and keep as much of the root ball intact as possible, tapping the base of the pot rather than yanking the plant out by its stem. Keep firming them in as you go, making sure there are no gaps or air pockets. If the roots of your plants have wound themselves around the bottom of the pot (pot-bound), gently spread them out before planting.

For tips on how to grow vegetables in containers see IDEA 15, *Small but perfectly formed*. IDEA 43, *Small trees for small gardens*, gives further ideas for trees in pots.

Try another idea...

'Plants in pots are like animals in a zoo – they're totally dependent on their keepers.'
JOHN VAN DE WATER (US gardening writer)

Defining idea...

Your compost should finish about 3cm below the rim to allow for ample watering, which should also be your next job. Finally, add a layer of gravel both for decorative and practical reasons – it helps to retain moisture.

Bulbs are perfect for pots and growing tulips in containers allows you to appreciate their magnificence close up, and increases the chance of a 100% success. But you can grow most plants in containers – annuals, perennials, grasses, shrubs, climbers, vegetables and herbs, even small trees will be quite happy – as long as you look after them. And that's the key.

CONSTANT CARE

Plants in containers need regular attention and regular watering – rain isn't enough to keep them going (even in the winter you need to keep an eye on the dryness of the compost). Pellets of slow-release fertiliser pressed into the soil are a good idea too, although the plants will also appreciate a fortnightly dose of tomato feed in summer.

Deadheading, replacing plants that are past their prime and checking pots for any pests, such as slugs or weevils, that have had the audacity to climb in, should all become part of your maintenance routine.

Q **I fancy a herb garden but don't have the space. How will they fare in a pot?**

A *Very well. Try using a strawberry pot. Add plenty of grit and plant up each hole with your favourite herbs. Put in both the curly and broad-leaved parsleys near the bottom leaving the sun seekers, like thyme and sage, near the top. Then you can place it right outside the kitchen door or on the patio near the barbeque. Herbs do well in hanging baskets too.*

Q **Trees in containers – you're joking aren't you?**

A *Not at all. The ones to go for are those that are naturally dwarf or slow growing, or which won't mind regular pruning. It also means that you can grow trees that won't thrive in the rest of the garden, such as tender ones. Citrus fruit grows well in large pots and you can wheel them inside for winter. Among good container trees for sunny spots are the bay laurel (Laurus nobilis) and the common fig (Ficus carica), while for shade you could try the evergreen Pittosporum tenuifolium.*

How did it go?

181

42

The herb garden

Why choose freeze dried when you could be picking fresh herbs every time you need them?

The beauty of herbs is that they'll go anywhere — the corner of a mixed bed, a container or hanging basket, or just dotted around the vegetable patch, where they may even become important companion plants to other crops.

Choosing which herbs to grow is a matter of taste in more ways than one. Grow what you enjoy cooking with but consider colour, form and structure too. Many herbs are perennials that you can leave in the ground to do their bit year after year, with just a haircut in autumn. They're easily propagated from cuttings too.

Herbs also throw up some attractive flowers, although the effort they put into doing this does detract from their core business of producing tasty leaves. The best time to harvest herbs is in the early morning.

SUN WORSHIPPERS

Many herbs naturally grow on the sun-baked, well-drained soils of Mediterranean countries, so choose a bright spot – near to the kitchen door if you can.

Here's an idea for you... **Bay (*Laurus nobilis*) responds well to being clipped – right down to the ground if necessary. So why not train (or buy) one as a standard, leaving room for other herbs below. Or place two in pots at your house entrance for a noble effect! Each time you prune save the clippings for the kitchen.**

Thyme, marjoram, basil, sage, rosemary and bay all need sun, which helps to improve their flavour, although the last two also enjoy a bit of shelter. For shady spots try chives, parsley, mint and chervil.

Most herbs prefer light, fertile soil and if you garden on chalk you're laughing. Mint and parsley like moister conditions. They do well in containers too – arrange those that enjoy the same type of conditions together.

MINT CONDITIONS

Mint is worthy of special mention for its wide range of uses and varieties. Its familiar flavour is used in soups, chopped up for mint sauce, and no new potato should be cooked without it. Pouring boiling water over a few sprigs in a jug makes an effective digestive at the end of a meal.

Unlike many herbs, mint likes its soil rich and moist and it will cope with light shade or sun. Give it plenty of room but, as a rule, better flavoured mints are less rampant.

To choose a variety that you like, pick a bit and taste it. The one your granny used to grow was probably *M. spicata* 'Moroccan' or 'Tashkent', with many blue/mauve flowers much loved by bees. Apple mint, with distinctive furry leaves, has good flavour for mint sauce. For purely aromatic reasons – and you can cook with them too – grow Eau de Cologne, lime or chocolate mint on or near the terrace.

MIXED HERBS

Below are some to consider for your plot.

- Basil – annual herb much used in Italian and French cooking, and with tomatoes. It likes full sun but loses its flavour when frozen.
- Sage – as much a hardy evergreen shrub as a herb. A quick trim in spring and after flowering will keep it vigorous, but don't cut back into old wood. Has purple-blue flower spikes in early to mid-summer and grey or purple foliage.
- Thyme – a dwarf evergreen that you can harvest all-year round. It needs good drainage and will grow happily in cracks between paving slabs. There are green and gold forms.
- Rosemary – at its best in full sun, it will grow into a small shrub and makes a good, low-growing hedge around the front of a bed of herbs. There's also a cascading form to grow over a low wall or raised bed.
- Tarragon – not fully hardy so make sure you give it some winter protection from frost. For taste, grow the French variety.
- Parsley – actually classed as a hardy biennial but, for the best flavour, treat it as an annual. Low growing with curly or broad-leaved varieties. Start if off in early spring under a cloche. Pouring boiling water over the ground first can help the seeds on their way. Keep some seeds back to sow in July and September to take you through to the year end.
- Chervil – an annual with a parsley-like flavour that can be sown anytime between April and August. Likes moist but well-drained soil. Doesn't work as a dried herb.

To learn more about how herbs can help control pests in your garden see IDEA 32, *Alright mate*.

Try another idea...

'Herbs are the friend of the physician and the pride of cooks.'
CHARLEMAGNE

Defining idea...

- Chives – throw up their mauve balls of colour in early summer and are great for the front of a bed or along a path. Deadhead if you don't want it to self seed.
- Marjoram (or oregano) – beloved of pizza makers. A hardy perennial that has small mauve flowers in summer. Its bright golden-green leaves and clump-forming habit make it a good ground cover plant for the front of the shrub bed. Trim back in autumn and divide every three years.
- Fennel – a tall, striking plant with umbels of tiny yellow flowers and wispy bright green or bronze foliage.
- Dill – similar to fennel with feathery blue-green leaves on tall stems. Use fresh or dried.
- Coriander – you can eat the leaves and the ripe seeds of this low-growing annual.

Of the more unusual herbs, horseradish is good value because not only do you get to use its hot, fiery root for sauce, but the young leaves can be used in a salad. A pot may be ideal though, as once planted you will never get rid of the root.

How did it go?

Q My mint's gone mad! Can you help?

A *Mint is invasive and best grown in a pot, sunken into the soil. (Make sure there are some drainage holes.) For the best results, cut mint right back in autumn and watch out for mildew.*

Q My fennel's done well but the seeds don't really taste of fennel. Why's that?

A *Chances are you've planted it too close to either some dill or coriander and it's cross-pollinated. This has a dramatic and adverse affect on its flavour.*

43

Small trees for small gardens

Choosing the right tree for your garden is possibly the most important horticultural decision you can make. So it pays to pick the right one.

We love trees, with their dark, distinctive silhouettes, their spirit-lifting blossom, ever-changing leaves, and crabby, rough bark. They're beautiful.

So we were justifiably mortified when our neighbour explained that the roots of one of our sycamores was playing havoc with his garage door. He suggested it should come down. We were hesitant and phoned the council, hoping to find a tree preservation order had been slapped on it. It hadn't, and we were forced to call the tree surgeons in.

In retrospect, the neighbour was probably right. Some trees can outgrow their welcome, and the felling of the sycamore has let much more light into an already slightly gloomy north-facing plot.

We did our bit by replacing it with a silver birch and a simple holly, just two of a huge range of trees we could have chosen. For early blossom we could have plumped for a flowering cherry (*Prunus*), crab apple (*Malus*) or the delicate pink blossom of the

187

Here's an idea for you...

Still scared about what those roots could do to your foundations? Then how about growing a tree in a pot? The maidenhair tree (*Ginkgo biloba*) is a good choice, with its delightfully random habit and unusual fan-shaped leaves, which turn golden yellow in autumn (it's also been around for over 160 million years!) Choose a minimum 40-litre pot (if it's terracotta, line it with plastic) and fill with a mixture of soil (loam) and compost. Keep well watered and in spring top dress with fertiliser. Review the pot size every five years.

ornamental plum (*Prunus cerasifera* 'Nigra'), one of the first to appear, and with the flowers closely followed by deep purple leaves. A rose-pink flowered version of the wild hawthorn, *Crataegus laevigata* 'Paul's Scarlet', is also well worth considering for a small garden.

In spring, magnolia is hard to beat, although if you garden on chalk your only choice is the multi-stemmed *Magnolia stellata*. It's hardy but in cold areas be prepared to cover it with fleece at night to protect the starry white flowers from frost.

Two other possibilities with spring colour are lilac (*Syringa*), in its white, mauve and purple forms, and laburnum, which although poisonous is still a striking, slow-growing tree with graceful, yellow hanging flowers (racemes).

In summer a tree can be enjoyed close-up, so it needs to either complement surrounding plants or be a stunner in its own right, such as the variegated acer (*A. platanoides* 'Drummondii'), with its single straight stem and fabulous green, edged-white maple leaves.

The false acacia (*Robinia pseudoacacia* 'Frisia') has acid green foliage and looks good in a sheltered, sunny spot, and the honey locust (*Gleditsia triacanthos* 'Sunburst') has unusual, finely divided green and yellow leaves.

AUTUMN AND WINTER WONDERS

Autumn colour is a real boost as summer disappears. And the secret of those rusty reds and cheery yellows is all in the soil; the more acidic it is, the better the autumn colour.

See IDEA 10, *Support network*, for advice on staking your tree and why you should grow a small clump of hazel.

Try another idea...

Maples (*Acer*) are renowned for their autumnal colour but many grow into monsters so choose carefully. The Japanese maples are relatively small, and A. *japonicum* 'Vitifolium' or A. *palmatum* 'Atropurpureum' grow well if sheltered from the wind.

For a tough, uncomplicated little tree, with vibrant autumn colour, choose the Stag's horn sumach (*Rhus typhina* 'Laciniata'). or the crab apple (*Malus* 'Golden Hornet') that has both golden fruit and yellow leaves in autumn.

Trees in winter are a dramatic feature of the sky line but there's interest close up too. *Acer pensylvanicum* is not called the snake bark acer for nothing! The spindle tree (the deciduous *Euonymous*), on acid soil, turns flame red in autumn and its red berries, shaped like a cardinal's hat, are a favourite with robins in winter.

Some trees have it all and are interesting for most of the year. *Amelanchier lamarckii* is an easy-growing small tree, absolutely hardy, with pretty white spring blossom, black fruits in summer (again a meal ticket for the birds) and good autumn tints.

'Except during the nine months before he draws breath, no man manages his affairs as well as a tree does.'
GEORGE BERNARD SHAW

Defining idea...

Conifers are an extremely diverse group of trees: soft or spiky, with green, yellow, bronze or blue foliage; upright and slim; spreading or weeping. Be sure to choose a slower growing type, such as the blue-grey *Chamaecyparis lawsoniana* 'Columnaris', the lace-bark pine *Pinus bungeana* or the golden cedar *Cedrus deodara* 'Aurea'.

TREAD CAREFULLY

Returning to the sycamore we now find that this is no more than a weed in most people's minds, so pull out all those little self-sown seedlings whilst they are small.

Unless your garden resembles a Capability Brown-style park, avoid planting potential giants. Leave beech, oak and ash to the countryside. But birch is a possibility. Plant three white-stemmed silver birches for a mini woodland glade, providing dappled shade for spring bulbs, foxgloves and hellebores.

Fascinating and popular once again, the monkey puzzle tree (*Araucaria araucaria*) is certainly different. It is hardy, will grow in any free-draining soil but may take ten years to reach 1.5m. After that, however, it will add 30cm a year! Bearing in mind it could last for 200 years, only plant it where there's plenty of room to grow.

Q **I've got a couple of trees but there's room for one or two more – where should I get them from, and when?**

How did it go?

A *Go to a nursery, where you can check the root system and confirm its predicted height, spread and rate of growth with an expert. If you're buying a bare-rooted tree, plant it when it's dormant. Container grown trees can be planted at any time, as long as it is not frosty or during a dry spell.*

Q **I've bought the trees, now what?**

A *Dig a hole large enough for the roots to spread out, loosen the soil on the sides and bottom, and add plenty of compost. Put the stake in first, and then place the tree so that, when the hole is filled in, the soil will be level with the old soil mark on the tree. Use a cane across the hole to check this. You can also add some slow-release fertiliser into the removed soil. Water well and keep the tree moist throughout its first couple of years. Keep an area of 1m around the tree free from weeds, and mulch in spring. As a general rule, tree roots are as long as the tree is tall so always plant them well away from buildings.*

44

Whispering grass don't tell the trees

Add movement and sound to your garden with the waving and rustling of ornamental grasses.

Visit a garden centre and it's hard to ignore the ranks of ornamental grasses. They seem the perfect filler for gappy borders, a ready-made solution for beds that need a bit of perking up.

Yet grasses are notoriously tricky to place, mainly because they're more informal than most garden plants, with features that can dramatically change as the seasons pass. What may start out as a low-growing tuft can suddenly explode into a riot of elegant spires. Some grasses need protection to flower well, and even then it may not happen until late summer or early autumn. And while some like moist, dappled shade others thrive in open sunny conditions.

SUPER GRASS

The list of grasses is long (and so are some of the names) but if you can get to know a handful and place them well, you'll have added a new dimension to your planting.

Here's an idea for you...

Be bold and brave and bring a little bit of the prairies to your garden by putting a whole area down to ornamental grasses. In this way you can overcome many of the difficulties of placing grasses by planting them together – perhaps where the garden becomes less formal, such as round a pond, or in a sunny, sheltered spot.

Bearing in mind the conditions they need, select a group of grasses of varying heights and try to group as many of one type together for maximum impact, such as seven plants of three varieties, rather than three each of seven different types.

To play to their strengths, marry grasses with contrasting plants. One winning combination we've come across is pairing the rust-coloured pheasant grass (*Stipa arundinacea*) with the erect shape and strong colour of red-hot pokers (*Kniphofia*); and the bold, flat leaves of hosta or bergenia complement the upright growth of *Calamagrostis*, with its fluffy flower heads that stiffen and cling on right through winter.

The sedges (*Carex*) love the damp, so here you can use their arching stems to soften the edges of a pond or pool – golden or striped leaves reflect best in the water, and *C. elata* 'Aurea' looks particularly good overhanging the water's edge. Other less fussy customers include hair grass (*Deschampsia cespitosa*), a tussocky evergreen with tall flower stalks that bear tiny shimmering flowers in June. It copes with sun or shade and thrives in moist soil. The variegated leaves of ribbon grass (*Phalaris*), commonly known as gardener's garters, are great for ground cover and it's quite happy with its feet in shallow water.

HIGH, WIDE AND HANDSOME

Some of the tallest grasses like the driest conditions. *Miscanthus sinensis* has banded, variegated or white-veined leaves. It's a well-behaved, medium-sized grass until late autumn, when it shoots up 2m-high flower stalks. These, of course, can be left on to catch the frost and enhance the winter garden. *Stipa gigantea*, as the name suggests, is another tall, bulky plant with oat-like feathery flowers that appear in early summer.

But the daddy of them all is pampas grass (*Cortaderia*) reaching some 3m in height. Its late-flowering architectural plumes seem to be a resident feature in the front gardens of any house built in the 1970s. Used as specimen plants in the past, why not try placing it at the back of the border as a foil for other upright, more colourful plants? Protect the crown in winter and strim off the previous year's growth, dividing if necessary in early spring.

IDEA 25, *Red alert – with a touch of orange, yellow, amber ...,* suggests other autumn plants to complement your grasses.

Try another idea...

FULL FRONTAL

Not all grasses are leggy monsters and there's a good selection for the front of the border too. Quaking grass (*Briza*) has blue-green foliage and dainty flowers in June, it is hardy and favours a well-drained site in full sun. But bear in mind that it self-seeds like mad.

The small, soft bottle-brush flowers of *Pennisetum orientale* will only appear in July if given a hot, sunny, sheltered position, on light, sandy or chalky soil. Finicky maybe but it looks great flowering over the path or lawn edge.

Another candidate is *Hakonechloa macra* 'Aureola', which starts off with brilliant yellow leaves in April that later become striped with green, before a flush of red in autumn.

'At no time does it look so perfect as in the evening, before and after sunset, when the softened light imparts a mistiness to the crowding plumes, and the traveller cannot help fancying that the tints, which then seem richest, are caught from the level rays of the sun, or reflected from the coloured vapours of the after glow.'
CHRISTOPHER LLOYD on pampas grass

Defining idea...

Three other exceptional low-to-medium grasses, which can jazz up your planting, include the bright yellow-leaved *Milium effusum*, better known as Bowles' golden grass. It prefers semi-shade and acts as a perfect foil to blue-flowered plants such as forget-me-nots or bluebells.

In complete contrast there's the low-growing, black, grass-like *Ophiopogon planiscapus* 'Nigrescens'. Plant this where it will show up – in gravel or amongst plants with golden flowers or foliage. *Festuca glauca* is a bright blue grass, forming a low clump with slightly taller flower stalks. Don't give it too rich a soil and place it with grey or silver leafed plants, or on its own.

How did it go?

Q I never know when to move or cut down grasses. Any tips?

A *It depends upon the grass but as a rule only plant or divide grasses when they're active. This will mean leaving those that need warm temperatures to come into growth, until late spring/early summer. Cut down flower stalks and old growth on deciduous grasses in spring, at the very first sign of the new shoots appearing.*

Q Is it true that if my pampas grass gets too big I can set the centre on fire?

A *You can, but think about the mess you'll be left with! Instead, try digging it up and dividing it. Remember to do this when the plant is visibly growing, and wear gloves as protection against the sharp-edged leaves.*

45

The wow factor

Big, bold and quite often just a little bit frightening. Are you brave enough to let architectural plants into your garden?

Is your herbaceous border crying out for more? Even chilled out, informal planting sometimes needs a full stop, a punctuation mark to draw in the eye before leading you off to take in the surrounding plants. True, pergolas, pots and statues give interest but, whether pointed, prickly or broad-leaved, there's nothing like a good architectural plant to provide a much-needed exclamation mark!

Used in twos (or more) to flank steps, entrances or pathways, they entice you in; you want to know what's round the corner. And their geometrical shapes fit both traditional and modern designs. The green architecture of clipped hedges and topiary has been used for centuries to form walls and pillars, themselves containing softer, more decorative planting. But shaped and sculptured plants are equally at home in the contemporary garden. In fact, they're essential.

Here's an idea for you... **How about a bit of architectural lawn sculpture? By setting the mower blades at differing levels you can cut a low-level maze or pattern into your lawn. Hours of fun, effective to look at, and easy to do.**

ON GUARD

Sword-like leaves, whether upright or arching, add drama to a garden. Take the strappy leaves of phormiums and yuccas – both striking on their own in pots, or shooting out of a bed of low growing plants. Try surrounding the bronze *Phormium tenax* with hellebores in spring and orange nasturtiums to trail through it in summer, and you'll create something altogether more exciting.

Equally arresting is a strategically placed *Yucca gloriosa* exploding out of a golden horizontal conifer (*Juniperus x media* 'Carberry Gold'). It's an effective contrast that increases the impact of the already striking yucca, which may, if it's in the mood, also decide to flower, producing a fantastic vertical spire of creamy bell-shaped blooms. Both phormiums and yuccas are hardy if sheltered. Much more tender is the weird, spiky foliage of aloe and agave. Their succulent rosettes, which can be up to 2m across, need temperatures of 5° or above and full sun to survive. You may have to wait 50 years for the agave to flower – on a 2m tall stem – but don't be too impatient as they die soon afterwards!

For a paved or gravel area that needs a bit of vertical interest try *Sisyrinchium striatum*. It's easy to grow and pushes up stalks of small creamy flowers, opening in the sun from amongst its iris-like leaves. A great self-seeder too.

A PRICKLY PRESENCE

Thistles, in the right place, can be an evocative sight, especially the ghostly grey, cobweb-strewn Scotch thistle (*Onopordum acanthium*). Its sculptured form fits best at the back of a border, against a darker fence or hedge. A biennial, it will take two years to reach its 1.8m. The cardoon (*Cynara cardunculus*) is similar but slightly less ghostly. It's a perennial too, with purple thistle flowers that are a bit larger than its Scottish cousin.

IDEA 50, *Frills and fronds*, covers another striking group of plants, and IDEA 23, *Good enough for pandas*, talks you through the different bamboos.

Try another idea...

Sea Holly (*Eryngium maritimum*) and the biennial Miss Willmott's Ghost (*Eryngium giganteum*) are prickly plants of more modest proportions, but nonetheless striking with their bristly leaves and blue flowers, which are loved by bees and hoverflies.

HAVE A BANANA

The banana (*Musa basjoo*) needs space to unfurl its wide, pale-green fringed leaves but it's winter-hardy if wrapped up against the frost. Cannas, with fabulous paddle-shaped leaves, takes less room but will need digging up and bringing inside over winter. For a taste of the Mediterranean, plant in groups with other hot-coloured perennials. The fan palm (*Trachycarpus fortunei*), which can grow to tree-like proportions with fans up to 1m wide, can stand temperatures down to –5°.

BROAD-LEAVED GIANTS

Apparently, during World War II, gunnera were grown on railway embankments to hide the tracks below from enemy bombers. This is a garden giant that means business and one of

'One of the charms of today's designs is that there are fewer preconceptions as to how a garden should look, so native plants with strong forms as well as exotic-looking subjects from sub-tropical climates are frequently included in the layout to add an element of surprise and challenge.'
JILL BILLINGTON, garden designer, lecturer and author

Defining idea...

the best known is *Gunnera manicata*, a 2m-high giant, with leaves up to 1.8m wide. It likes the damp, but keep the crown protected in winter with old dried leaves.

Scaling things down a bit, but in the same wet conditions, try *Rodgersia pinnata* 'Superba', with its reddish star-shaped leaves, and *Hosta sieboldiana* var. *elegans* with its grey-blue textured leaves, arching 50cm off the ground.

How did it go?

Q   It's all very well if you've got acres to garden but how can I use architectural plants in a small garden without them overwhelming everything else?

A   *Use them to increase the sense of space by playing tricks with perspective. Two lines of box balls can make the garden seem longer than it is. They look great topped with snow in winter and can be easily grown from cuttings (start them off in the veg plot and in a couple of years you can plant them in situ). They do well in pots and can be moved around for a different effect. To lengthen the garden use the Italian cypress (Cupressus sempervirens Stricta group), eventually reaching 10m, or the more modest 5m Juniperus communis 'Compressa', to provide tall, slim columns to draw the eye to the far part of the garden.*

Q   I have been given a cordyline. Will it perform like the phormiums and yuccas – it looks the same?

A   *Yes, it does have the same broad arching leaves but it is a little daintier and not so hardy. Why not get a second one and plant up two contrastingly curvaceous pots, to flank an entrance. This way you can move them into a light, frost-free place in winter.*

46

Up the garden path

Paths provide your garden's arterial network, but think more winding B roads than motorways, with patios as the country pub.

Paths and patios are a mixture of taste and necessity, but even a small garden can benefit from some form of hard landscaping, whether it's a paved area by the back door, or some strategically placed slabs as stepping stones across the lawn.

What often puts people off is the cost, but with a bit of imagination and a spot of hard graft you can add structure and a touch of mystery to your garden.

ON THE RIGHT TRACK

There are no hard and fast rules when it comes to choosing a path. Use shingle, bricks, crazy-paving and, of course, grass. If you have a few zigzagging across your garden, think variety of materials in the context of the area they are passing through.

Here's an idea for you... **Acquire the reputation of a skip scavenger. A builder's skip is home to old bricks, pipes and every conceivable kind of timber. It's become something of a trait to heave perfectly usable items into skips and then spend hours in DIY stores buying something virtually identical. Keep your eyes skinned and you need never purchase a brick or piece of wood again.**

Concrete, once laid, is easy to maintain and weed free but it does have a fearful permanency about it. A friend recently thought about extending a favourite border but was thwarted by a bed of concrete, and had no option but to scrap the plans or head off to the nearest hire and sale store for a pneumatic drill.

Crazy paving gets a bad press. Although it's another of those faddy ideas that smacks of the 1970s, like conifers and rockeries, it's actually pretty easy to lay and extremely versatile. You can simply bed it in grit or sand and only need to lay hardcore and mortar in exceptional circumstances, such as when it's earmarked as a driveway. Even for a patio, just bed them firmly in and grow rock-loving plants in the crevices. The sword-shaped leaves of sysirinchiums will give upright interest whilst the New Zealand burr (*Acaena*), the small flowered sedums (*S. acre* or *S. spathulifolium*) and houseleek (*Sempervivum*) are mat forming.

If the creative juices are really flowing, use the cracks to plant up a mini herb garden. Thyme and chives will take root in a little well-drained soil. And the occasional inadvertent kick will do them no harm, and give off a pleasant smell to boot.

For winding paths, it's hard to beat shingle, with its soft blend of beige and browns. As for laying it, just slash the bag and spread, but you will need to contain it otherwise it will disappear into the very border it's intended to show off. Choosing the ideal side support is important, and while a metal strip is effective and lasts forever, pliable strips of treated timber are a bit more discrete. For the truly artistic, try bricks on their ends leaning at 45° like falling dominoes.

See **IDEA 41, *How to get the most from your containers,* for how to dress up your patio.**

Try another idea...

As for weeds, a plastic membrane will discourage the worst but the shingle on top does have a tendency to rut and slide. Otherwise, your path will never be totally weed free. You could spray with a weed killer but an alternative is to give it a thorough weeding and keep on top of it, picking out any new weeds that dare to appear.

Bricks are a personal favourite when it comes to paths. They obviously have an immediate link with a brick-built house (presuming they're the same colour) and, although individually they're a pretty basic geometric shape, they can be brought together to form some stunning swirling shapes.

However, before attempting to recreate an elaborate mosaic on the ground, consider a few simple brick paths to split up your vegetable plot, or as a hard area by the compost bins.

'I gave the four end beds a circular pattern, with paths running through so that you can walk right round and savour the scent of each plant on your way'
ROSEMARY VEREY

Defining idea...

If you go for a grass path, calculate the width and then add some more, lest you turn the air blue when you first try and run the mower over it, only to succeed in beheading your carefully planted summer bedding. You wouldn't be the first person to create a path that's too narrow to mow.

PATIO POWER

Unless you've got special building skills, try to treat the patio as a bigger, wider path, which uses the same materials as mentioned above. But remember that major construction tends to introduce formal lines, which can jar with the rest of your garden.

Just a few tips if you wish to lay your own patio. Make sure the ground is very firm – no need for hardcore. Set the slabs on blobs of mortar – five per paving slab. Press or tamp the slabs into place, making sure they are level. If laying a patio up to grass, set the slabs slightly below grass level to allow the mower to pass over easily.

Whatever materials you use, the size, quantity and placing of pots, troughs and ornaments make all the difference to a patio. And don't restrict planting to summer alone as the patio is the ideal spot for a bit of R&R at any time of the year.

Q **I've tried a brick path but many of them broke up or flaked after one winter. What's going on?**

How did it go?

A *Bricks will break if laid on uneven ground, so bed them firmly in sand. Some bricks are softer than others and are more likely to absorb water, freeze and flake. If your brick path is confined to the vegetable patch, the occasional scarred brick is fine and changing the odd one isn't too arduous. If you want a pristine path, use harder and therefore less porous bricks.*

Q **I have gone for mainly grass but those paths in constant use suffer from worn patches in the summer. Can it be helped?**

A *Many nurseries and some garden centres offer a variety of grass seed. Seek out the bin marked 'hard wearing suitable for children's play area'.*

Q **You mention using stone patio materials but I would prefer to lay decking. Is this as easy?**

A *Getting decking right depends on building a strong, level structure. This can be tricky and probably needs a professional touch. Large garden centres stock a wide variety of decking materials – including non-slip, easy-fix squares.*

47

Common diseases

Determined diseases will breach the best-laid defences if they put their minds to it. Here's how to lessen the impact of some of the most virulent.

Turn to the disease section of any decent gardening tome and the scale of the problem you're up against is monumental. From apple scab to tulip fire, neck rot to stem canker, it's a frightening list.

On the basis that prevention is better than cure, you can help stop diseases spreading round your garden with a few simple measures. Garden hygiene is crucial, so make sure that washing flower pots and seed trays before sowing becomes part of your annual routine. Likewise, your greenhouse needs disinfecting every winter, and tools that have come into contact with diseased vegetation should be scrubbed in boiling water.

Clearing up dead and diseased leaves as they fall is also vital. They should be bagged up immediately to stop the spores spreading, and then either binned or burnt.

Here's an
idea for
you...

Crop rotation can help prevent the build up of pests and diseases in the vegetable plot. When buying a new tree or fruit bush, check whether it's resistant to the common diseases that are likely to attack it.

Of course, the more healthy and vigorous your plants, the more likely they are to successfully fight off a disease, so make sure you know what conditions they like before putting them in the ground. And keep checking them once they've become established, so that you can nip diseases and infestations in the bud.

A range of organic fungicides and pesticides is available, the difference being that they are derived from plants and other natural products that will break down quickly rather than linger in the ecosystem.

Bordeaux mixture is a finely ground concoction of copper sulphate and slaked lime, dissolved to form a fungicidal spray that controls fungus on fruits and blight on vegetables and perennials. Sulphur can be used to control powdery mildew. There are many proprietary and branded varieties too.

But, before you get trigger happy with your sprays and powders, these products can still have a harmful effect on the garden's beneficial insects. Instead, they're best used as a last resort, or alternatively as a quick blast when you first spot a problem, to stop it getting out of hand.

Here are some suggestions for coping with some of the most common diseases.

- *Grey mould.* Strawberries, and most other soft fruits, are a favourite of this rotting disease, which gets in through any bruised or damaged tissue. It thrives in cold, damp conditions and, although there's no organic cure, this is one of those diseases that can be prevented by good plant hygiene. Cut out infected growth as soon as you spot it and make sure there's a good airflow in and around the plant.

- *Rose black spot.* Sooty black marks begin to appear on rose leaves, turning them yellow and eventually causing them to fall prematurely. Worryingly, it can also spread to buds and stems. Remove and burn fallen leaves straight away, as this is where the fungi will overwinter. Over-feeding with nitrogen-rich fertilisers can also exacerbate the problem but there are plenty of resistant varieties, while shrub roses are naturally less susceptible. Curiously, polluted air will help control black spot.

- *Powdery mildew.* Many plants, including roses, apples and asters, are susceptible to this white powder, which is caused by a fungus and appears on leaves and shoots. It's caused by over-crowding and a lack of water getting to the roots, hence the fact that it thrives in dry, warm conditions. To cure it, cut out and burn all infected growth, and then give the plant a good water and dust with sulphur.

- *Blight.* This disease attacks potatoes and tomatoes. In damp conditions, brown and yellow patches begin to appear on the leaves. Spores can then be washed off into the soil and into contact with the tubers, or onto the fruit, causing them to rot. At the first sign of blight in potatoes, cut off all the haulms (stalks) about ten days before harvest. This should stop it spreading. In future years

For more on the pests that inhabit the garden see IDEA 51, *Pests.*

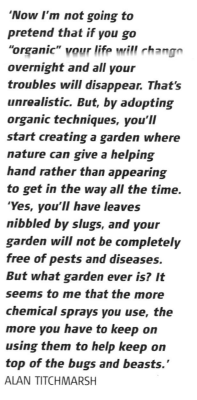

Try another idea...

'Now I'm not going to pretend that if you go "organic" your life will change overnight and all your troubles will disappear. That's unrealistic. But, by adopting organic techniques, you'll start creating a garden where nature can give a helping hand rather than appearing to get in the way all the time. 'Yes, you'll have leaves nibbled by slugs, and your garden will not be completely free of pests and diseases. But what garden ever is? It seems to me that the more chemical sprays you use, the more you have to keep on using them to help keep on top of the bugs and beasts.'
ALAN TITCHMARSH

Defining idea...

earthing up can protect potatoes. With tomatoes the picture isn't so hopeful but spraying with Bordeaux mixture may help.

■ *Clubroot*. This can take hold of your brassicas in the veg patch but will also set about wallflowers in the border, given half a chance. This disease is so easily spread that, if you own an allotment that's infected, using the same tools or boots in your own garden will spread it. In short, the roots become distorted, the plant withers and eventually dies. It can be eradicated over time through crop rotation, and liming the soil can help. As soon as you find an infected plant remove and destroy it, otherwise the roots will rot to a slimy mush, releasing millions of spores into the soil.

How did it go?

Q   Anything organic I can use to clean the greenhouse?

A   *Sulphur candles can be left to smoke out pests and diseases from the greenhouse during winter. There are also several organic, citrus-based disinfectants on the market that don't harm plants or wildlife.*

Q   Why is it that as soon as my seedlings poke their heads above the soil they seem to give up the ghost?

A   *Sounds like damping off. It's caused by a parasitic fungus that thrives in wet and overcrowded conditions. There's nothing you can do with the seedlings that have succumbed, but in future sow the seeds thinly into a sterilised seed compost (the fresher this is the more sterile it will be) and make sure there's good ventilation. Try watering the seed trays from below too.*

48

A place for everything, and everything in its place

From sun worshippers to shade lovers, the key to a blooming garden is giving your plants the conditions they love.

Some plants will grow just about anywhere, a band of tough, all-round performers such as lady's mantle (*Alchemilla mollis*), dead nettle (*Lamium*) and the frost-hardy *Tellima grandiflora* which, despite its insignificant flowers, has foliage that adds autumn colour to any garden.

Other plants are more choosy and will only flourish if you take the time and effort to plant them in the right position. Shoehorn them into a spot that's too sunny or too dark and at best they'll struggle, at worst they'll end up on the compost heap.

To get the best from your plants, and make the most of your money, you need to know the conditions they enjoy. Before embarking on a spending spree it helps if you have a particular spot of the garden in mind, then you know exactly the conditions you're buying for.

Here's an idea for you... **Always carry a notepad with you, whether you're visiting a garden or simply out walking. Note down plants you like the look of, and if you don't know the name ask, or write down a description. Record the conditions in which they're planted and the date, if they're in flower. Of course you may get lucky and persuade the gardener to give you a cutting!**

If a particular plant has caught your eye, then try looking it up in a plant encyclopaedia before you set off to the nursery. The plant's label will also detail its requirements, listing its preferences when it comes to sun or shade, soil type, drainage and shelter.

Sometimes you can create a microclimate in your garden by introducing different soil, improving drainage, using other plants for shelter, or cutting them back to introduce more light. But it's best to force as little as possible and far better to go with a plant's natural flow.

SUN WORSHIPPERS

Just as we like to feel the sun on our backs, most plants enjoy the warming rays on their leaves. They need the sun to thrive. If their roots are kept moist (you can achieve this by making sure there are no gaps in your planting, which keeps evaporation to a minimum) most plants will stand quite high temperatures. After all, the classic herbaceous border is usually placed in full sun, because plants deprived of light will often lean, growing thin and straggly as they flop around in search of the sun.

Of course, it's not quite as straightforward as that. While large flowered clematis enjoy showing off their blooms in full sun, they insist on having their roots in the shade. If neighbouring plants can't supply this then rocks or slates at the base of the plant will do the job. Then there's the bulb *Nerine bowdenii*, which, you've guessed it, just loves to have its roots in the sun, at the bottom of a wall or fence, for example.

SHADE LOVERS

Plants suited to all-day-long shade are usually those with striking foliage – elephant's ears (*Bergenia cordifolia*) and hostas, with their broad leaves, the wide selection of ferns, and pulmonaria with its 'spilt milk' markings.

Fine dappled shade gives you a chance to grow flowering woodland plants like foxgloves, hellebores (*H. foetidus* and *H. orientalis*), violets, and Solomon's seal (*Polygonatum*) with its gracefully arching stems and white flowers.

The problem with shade under trees is that anything you plant has to compete for food and water with the tree itself. Early spring bulbs under a deciduous tree have a better chance, as they can bloom before the tree leaves deprive them of the light. Give them some extra feed (a sprinkle of bonemeal when the soil is not too dry) to swell the bulbs for next year.

If you have a problem area you could try the low-growing form of comfrey (*Symphytum grandiflorum*) as this is a 'thug' and seems to romp away in most conditions.

Two other plants with a particular liking for the shade are the climbing hydrangea (*Hydrangea petiolaris*), which has lush foliage and white blooms and is good at covering a north-facing wall, and the shrub *Philadelphus coronarius* 'Aureus'. This is a variation on the mock orange and, to keep its bright lime-green leaves, it needs to be grown in the shade.

Soil type also plays an important part in successful planting and IDEA 1, *Did the earth move?*, takes you through the merits of an acid or alkaline soil.

Try another idea...

'Odd as it may appear, a gardener does not grow from seed, shoot, bulb, rhizome or cutting but from experience, surroundings and natural conditions.'
KAREL CAPEK

Defining idea...

213

FROST – UNPREDICTABLE BUT DEADLY

A late frost in April or May is the gardening equivalent of a crash on the stock exchange – it can do untold damage, destroying new shoots, fruit tree blossom and flower buds. And, although the plants will usually recover, you'll have to wait another twelve months for flowers or fruit. Winter frosts can reap even more havoc, leaving all but the most hardy plants dead to the roots.

So it pays to know where the frost pockets are in your garden. If you've got a cold, open site, or a plot on a low-lying valley bottom or exposed, windy hillside, then don't be seduced by shrubs that are not *fully* hardy. Plants such as rock rose (*Cistus*), convolvulus, and witch hazel (*Hamamelis mollis*), as well as daphnes and hebes, won't survive a heavy frost. Instead, try planting them in the lee of a wall or alongside the house, for some extra protection.

How did it go?

Q How can I tell where the frost pockets are in my garden?

A *Next time you have a frost make a note of those parts of the garden where it lies undisturbed, and those in which it gradually clears.*

Q I planted some shrubs in the wrong place several years ago. Can I still move them?

A *You can usually get away with moving shrubs in spring or autumn. Keep as much soil on the root ball as possible, move directly to the new, larger planting hole, and then water, feed and prune if necessary.*

49

Upwardly mobile

Climbers bring a dynamic element to the gardens, eagerly taking up the challenge to scramble over any natural and man-made structure you put in their way.

Who can fail to love a climber? They're one of the most versatile groups of plants going, perfect for climbing over arches, rambling through trees and shrubs, and masking ugly buildings and blank walls. (They're also great for softening hard edges throughout the garden.)

But despite their wanderlust and tearaway reputation, climbers also need a certain degree of TLC. Indulge their foibles and their fads with careful planting, regular food and water, and the correct pruning, and the social climbers of the plant world will pay you back with a stunning array of colours.

The best border in the world can be ruined by a backdrop of rotting fence panels, garage roof or uninspiring wall. Enter those rampant runners like Russian vine (*Polygonum baldschuanicum*), also known as 'mile-a-minute', whose sprays of snowy white flowers can cloak a shed overnight

Here's an idea for you...

If you've got a north-facing wall that needs brightening up, the climbing hydrangea (*Hydrangea petiolaris*) is the answer. It will thrive in the shade and rapidly clothe a dark wall with lush green foliage and lacy white flower heads in summer. What's more, after a little initial persuasion, it will cling on all by itself.

Ivy (*Hedera*) is another garden staple, yet often overlooked for more exotic climbing cousins. But with foliage that ranges from dark green to bright gold, and berries that veer from black to cream, it can clamber over anything from tree stumps to outhouses, adding a verdant and mystical air as it goes.

Virginia creeper (*Parthenocissus quinquefolia*) is another well-known and energetic climber, much loved for its magnificent autumn colour.

Well worth growing too is the crimson glory vine (*Vitis coignetiae*), its large plate-sized leaves also turning a brilliant red in autumn.

Two clematis that verge on the monstrous side, are the scented, spring-flowering *C. montana*, and the evergreen *C. armandii*. Both are vigorous, and while they need plenty of room, they'll do any screening job asked of them.

One word of warning – as with all climbers on houses, make sure they're kept away from gutters and roof tiles.

ROMANTIC RAMBLINGS

Slightly less invasive are the honeysuckle, rambling rose and jasmine. Try the purple and cream flowered honeysuckle (*Lonicera periclymenum*) or the evergreen honeysuckle (*Lonicera japonica* 'Halliana'). Both have a delicious, subtle perfume. *Rosa banksiae* 'Lutea', with its masses of small yellow flowers is vigorous and needs a strong structure – preferably a tree – to attack. R. 'Felicité Perpetué' has clusters of creamy pink flowers and at 3.5m is more easily controlled. The climbing rose, R. 'Albertine', grows easily but within reason, with salmon buds opening to pale pink.

Idea 22, *It's been a good year for the roses*, introduces more climbing and rambling roses.

Try another idea...

At the turn of the year there's nothing so welcoming as the brave, bright yellow flowers of the winter flowering jasmine (*Jasminum nudiflorum*). The white flowered version (*J.officinale*), given a little shelter, will also romp away and scent the air in summer.

PRUNING FOR FLOWERS

Now people have devoted their lives to the clematis, and there are far more authoritative tomes on the plant than this one. But follow one basic rule and you're at least heading in the right direction. Clematis need to be pruned at the right time in order to encourage flowers.

'So when's the right time?', you may well ask. To which we can only reply: 'Read the label'.

Clematis come in three groups.

'A morning glory at my window satisfies me more than the metaphysics of books.'
WALT WITMAN

Defining idea...

- Group 1 includes *C. montana*, *C. macropetala*, *C. armandii*, *C. alpina* – those with small flowers that bloom in spring. These only require pruning when they get out of bounds. In which case be ruthless.
- Group 2 are the large-flowered beauties that perform in early to mid-summer. *C.* 'Nelly Moser', *C.* 'Marie Boisselot' and *C.* 'The President' for example. Prune these in early spring before new growth starts, remove any dead or damaged stems and cut the ends only, back to a strong pair of buds.

- Group 3 clematis flower towards the end of summer or in autumn on growth they have made during the year. Cut this group, including *C.* 'Jackmanii', *C. tangutica* and *C. viticella*, right down in January to the first pair of healthy buds.

Oh, and don't forget the wisteria, which also needs wooing, as well as pruning twice a year. In August cut back all the long, whippy shoots to six leaf buds, then in February cut these back further to just two. Drastic maybe, but as long as you keep the frost off, it will be well worth it.

FOR ONE YEAR ONLY

If you're worried about climbers getting triffid-like tendencies and taking over the whole show, grow some annuals. The cup and saucer vine (*Cobaea scandens*) provides quick cover and striking flowers from May to October, and Morning Glory (*Ipomoea*) – coming into flower in late summer – can be used to climb through and brighten up shrubs that have already done their bit.

Defining idea...

'**Climbers are invaluable in the small-space garden. Not only do they make it possible to enjoy plants for their own sake, without using up valuable ground space, but they can be used to soften visually hard structures or disguise ugly ones and, in conjunction with a pergola or openwork fencing, provide privacy, shade and shelter.**'
JOHN BROOKES

Plant a golden hop (*Humulus lupulus* 'Aureus') and it will cover an arch in a season with striking yellow foliage, plus a few hops as well. It's a perennial, dying back completely in winter but raring to go again the following spring. Grown with a dark red clematis (a group 3 type, by the way, which as you now know you prune in January) it makes a stunning combination.

Q **I now know how to prune my clematis but how do I prevent clematis wilt?**

How did
it go?

A *The scourge of many a gardener but it can be quite easily beaten. Dig a deep hole at least 40cm away from the wall or fence. Fill with compost, sprinkle in some fertiliser and plant the clematis leaning towards its support. Sink the clematis so the point where the shoots emerge is below ground level. Then, should it succumb to clematis wilt, it will regrow happily from beneath the soil. Keep it well watered – better to apply six buckets of water in one go than one a day for six days – and shade its roots with other plants or stones.*

Q **What type of support should I use for vigorous climbers?**

A *The strongest you can find! Always make sure the supports are well grounded and, if wooden, use treated timbers sunk into met posts. Having to dismantle a tangled climber in order to replace its support is a nightmare.*

50

Frills and fronds

There's a lot more to ferns than unpronounceable Latin names.

Shade loving, slug resistant, maintenance free. Goodness, oh how we love ferns. The way their fronds unfurl, the way they filter the light, the way they gracefully cling to walls and rocks. It's enough to make even the most sceptical gardener go weak at the knees.

They even pre-date just about anything else you're likely to be growing in your garden, and the fact that they'll grow where others fear to tread makes them a virtually indispensable plant.

GREAT FOLIAGE, SHAME ABOUT THE FLOWERS

OK, that's quite enough hyperbole, especially given it's a plant that doesn't actually produce any fruit or flowers. What you see is what you get with ferns, green foliage and a plant that, to a greater or lesser extent, is happy in moist, light shade.

Not that it hasn't got a troublesome streak, and you need to get to grips with the fact that different types of the same species prefer different pH levels in the soil.

Here's an idea for you...

For the busy gardener on the lookout for all-year-round interest, plant bulbs in between the ferns. Choose varieties that die down in the winter, and mix in some early spring bulbs. The fronds will cover the bulbs as they die back. If you feel adventurous, add in some easy-care plants with different leaf types such as hosta, elephant's ears (*Bergenia*), or small shrubs like the slow-growing, glossy dark green Sweet box (*Sarcoccoca*) or dwarf azaleas.

The oak fern (*Gymnocarpium*), for instance, has a variety G. *dryopteris* which prefers acid ground, and another, G. *robertianum*, which is a native of that most alkaline of habitats, the limestone pavement. So, as with so many plants, you need to read up on them, rather then just lumping them all together and hoping for the best.

Woodland ferns that are at home in moist, humus-rich acid soil include the small and delicate maidenhair fern (*Adiantum pedatum*) with its bright green leaves and black stems, all species of lady fern (*Athyrium*), the soft-textured shield fern (*Polystichum*), and *Blechnum* with its glossy green leaves on upright fertile fronds.

There are fewer lime lovers for alkaline soil but the Hart's tongue (*Asplenium scolopendrium*) will happily colonise a stone wall, living off the lime in the mortar. *Polypodium vulgare* is not fussy about soil *and* will tolerate drier conditions but resist the temptation to cut its fronds back. Let them fade and shrivel, as the new growth takes time to develop (with most other ferns you can cut them back when the fronds die off in autumn).

MIMICKING THE WILD

As is often the case, nature shows us where plants like to grow best. If you see ferns by a woodland stream, or squeezed into a split in the rock, make a note of the type and try recreating the surroundings in your garden.

Waterside ferns include the upright shuttlecock fern (*Matteuccia orientalis*) and the royal fern (*Osmunda regalis*) with its ostrich-feather fronds. On moist soil both are quite capable of reaching over 1m in height. The Sensitive fern (*Onoclea sensibilis*) is hardy although its fronds will disappear at the first sign of frost. It too likes a wet site and the young fronds start off a pretty pink in spring.

The common but handsome male fern (*Dryopteris filix-mas*) is tough and undemanding, settling into shady north-facing cracks and crevices, growing to 1.5m. The variety (*D. filix-mas crispa-cristata*) is crested and smaller at 0.5m.

IDEA 45, *The wow factor*, suggests other dramatic foliage to go with your ferns and IDEA 1, *Did the earth move?*, will help you determine your soil type.

Try another idea...

STICK IT WHERE THE SUN DON'T SHINE

The real beauty of ferns is that there's often a spot just right for them that's unsuitable for most other plants, such as a sheltered north-facing site at the bottom of a wall or hedge. Anywhere spring to mind? If so you could do a lot worse than dedicate it to the fern, and leave those feathery fronds to unfurl in peace. Just make sure it never gets waterlogged

To create a fernery, dig leaf mould, well-rotted compost or pine bark into the top layer of soil, along with some bonemeal. Avoid animal manure or artificial fertilisers as they're too rich.

**'Where the copse wood is the greenest
Where the fountain is the sheenest
Where the morning dew lies longest
There the Lady Fern grows strongest'**
SIR WALTER SCOTT

Defining idea...

On clay soil it may be necessary to improve the drainage by digging down two spits and adding rubble to the bottom. Mix grit into the top layer if necessary.

223

Plant the ferns in spring or autumn. Once underway they need little attention, no staking and no deadheading! All will relish an annual mulch of compost in spring and, in the cold areas, be prepared to cover the crowns in winter with some bracken leaves.

How did it go?

Q   To add height to my fernery I would like to plant the tree fern (*Dicksonia antarctica*). Is it hardy?

A   *This fashionable and statuesque plant, with tree-like proportions, has lacy fronds growing out of a stout trunk. It will survive the winter in a sheltered spot if its crown is thoroughly wrapped up against the cold.*

Q   You have helped me choose ferns for my soil but which ferns are evergreen?

A   *Ferns that keep their fronds over winter are known as 'wintergreen'. In the spring new fresh growth will take the place of the old fronds so there's a succession of green. Wintergreens include Asplenium, Polypodium vulgare, Polystichum, Blechnum, and Dryopteris affinis.*

Q   You say ferns are the almost perfect plants but are they easy to propagate?

A   *Ferns reproduce through spores, the minute, dust-like particles that grow on the outside of the plant, usually the back of the leaves. Athryium, Blechnum, Drypoteris, Matteuccia struthiopteris and Osmunda regalis are relatively easy to grow from spores. It is a bit fiddly but quite possible if you read up on it.*

51

Pests

Chemical-free pest control has come a long way since the days of the fly swatter.

The late doyen of British gardening, Geoff Hamilton, once wrote: 'I firmly believe, and indeed have proved to my own satisfaction, that chemical pest control is counter-productive.'

Hamilton reasoned that, despite years of bombarding commercial crops with chemicals, pests were more prevalent then ever, something he put down to the indiscriminate nature of most sprays, which were killing friend as well as foe.

What is more, it was the fast-breeding pests that were re-establishing themselves a lot quicker than the predators that hunted them.

It was something Hamilton didn't want to replicate in his own garden. He knew there was no quick fix to the problem but with a mixture of healthy plants, good soil, vigilance and the patience to allow the garden's ecosystem to reset its own balance, the ordered garden could once again be harmonised with nature.

Here's an idea for you... **Although earwigs eat aphids, they can do more damage than greenfly, feeding at night on flowers and buds. To catch them, fill a small plastic flower pot with straw and place it on top of a cane. Chances are the earwigs will be attracted to the pot as a refuge during the day, handily gathering together so you can collect and destroy them.**

So, how can green gardeners protect their crops?

BIOLOGICAL WARFARE

Whilst spraying roses with washing-up liquid and picking off caterpillars may be effective, a range of biological predators is now available that will thrive in the warm conditions of a greenhouse or conservatory. You can buy small vials of parasitic wasps, ladybird larvae and other tiny bugs to let loose on your pest-infested vegetation.

The whitefly, for instance, destroys tomatoes and peppers by leaving a sticky trail that attracts sooty moulds. Well, a tiny wasp called *Encarsia formosa* lays its eggs inside the immature whitefly, killing them at the same time. Red spider mites suck the sap from a variety of plants, causing them to wilt, but they can be defeated by the introduction of another predatory mite, *Phytoseiulus*. In the same way you can introduce *Aphidius* and *Aphidoletes* into your greenhouse or conservatory to control aphids.

Yellow glue traps hung close to the plant are also effective but of course may trap some non-harmful insects too.

Defining idea... **'A blank helpless sort of face, rather like a rose just before you drench it with DDT.'**
Author JOHN CAREY

BEETLE DRIVE

Back outside, vine weevils are among the most destructive of pests. While the adult beetles will nibble at leaves, it's the grubs that do the real damage, devouring the roots until the plant dies. But help is at hand in the form of a pathogenic nematode that can be watered into the soil to attack the milky white grubs.

Tackling slugs and snails is dealt with all on its own in IDEA 12, *Slugging it out.* Enjoy!

Try another idea...

Nematodes are also available to take on chafer grubs, leatherjackets and slugs. These biological controls are largely sold through mail order from the Internet, and to be effective you need to use them at exactly the correct time. But they are harmless to kids, pets and other wildlife.

There's little mistaking another destructive creature, the lily beetle, with its bright red body and black legs (the Cardinal beetle has the same colouring but is twice as big). Both the adult and grub feed on the leaves and flowers of lilies and fritillaries, and while they are one of those pests that are best picked off and destroyed, go carefully as the bugs are prone simply to drop off the leaves into the undergrowth as soon as they sense you coming. Lily beetles also overwinter as adults, so if you grow lilies in pots it pays to have a good rummage in the compost to hunt any out.

ALTERNATIVE REMEDIES

Hand picking is another simple way to keep on top of pests. Caterpillars on brassicas and nasturtiums can be dealt with in this way, while aphids are quite easily rubbed off buds and new shoots.

There's also a range of organic pesticides, most of which have been developed from plant extracts. Pyrethrum is effective against most insects, while Derris is effective on caterpillars. Neither is selective though, so should be used as a last resort.

'To hear some people talk of their garden you would think they were referring more to a battleground than to a place of peace and tranquility'
BERNARD SCHOFIELD, gardener, artist and writer

Defining idea...

Insecticidal soap kills the likes of aphids, whitefly, red spider mite, scale insects and mealy bugs. These soaps are harmless to humans, mammals, ladybirds and bees, but can damage some sensitive plants. A gentler alternative is soft soap, which can be used as a spray for aphids and red spider mite, but only hangs around for a day at most.

Add to these controls the likes of companion planting, encouraging more wildlife into your garden, making sure your plants aren't congested, and crop rotation, and suddenly the chemical-free gardener doesn't feel quite so alone.

 How did it go?

Q   I've nothing against squirrels, apart from the fact that they dig up and eat my *@^% bulbs! What can I do?

A   *Firstly, plant them deep. Then sprinkle cayenne pepper on liberally, re-cover with earth, and lace the soil around them with more pepper. Sit back and watch their faces as they start digging! Alternatively, chicken wire secured over the pot or bulb site will prevent digging.*

Q   My fruit trees have taken a right beating. How can I protect them?

A   *Grease bands round the trunks of fruit trees, tied on in autumn, can help stop the winter moth from climbing up to lay its eggs. You can also use traps to take care of the codling moth. The caterpillars will eat into pears and apples but you can catch the adult males before they breed using pheromone traps hung in the tree from the end of May. The moths will get caught on a sticky pad inside.*

52

Currant thinking

Add a tang to summer with easy-to-grow currants and gooseberries.

For over 200 years we've been using the vitamin C in blackcurrants to protect against colds, while gooseberries have been around since the thirteenth century. They reached their peak through the popular Gooseberry Clubs of the 1740s, when there was talk of goosegogs the size of hen's eggs.

Both gooseberries and currants are related, and require similar conditions. They're all good croppers, respond well with minimum care and can be 'trained' to take up less room. Yet when was the last time you saw a punnet of gooseberries in the shops, or redcurrants that weren't priced as if they'd been imported from the moon?

Here's an idea for you...

If you're really stuck for space, try planting a 'standard' gooseberry or redcurrant. Produced with bare stems to a height of about 1m, the tops are then pruned in the same way as the bush varieties. Standards look impressive and crop well, yet in a small garden allow other fruit or veg to be grown beneath. They do need strong and permanent staking though.

TURNING ON THE CURRANTS

With several different varieties of blackcurrant available, it pays to plant two or more bushes to ensure a good crop.

Blackcurrants relish an open, sunny site, sheltered from strong winds but where their roots can keep cool. Although hardy, the flowers can be damaged by frost so plant a late-flowering variety, like Ben Sarek or Baldwin, if you live in a frosty area. Where space is limited, try the compact-growing Blacksmith, while for an early crop there's the large fruited Laxton's Giant. Ben Hope is a mid-season variety that's resistant to big bud mite, the blackcurrant's main health risk.

For the best results plant two-year-old bushes between November and February, 1.5m apart, in a deep hole. Fill the bottom half with well-rotted manure and place the plant just below the original soil mark on the stems to encourage new shoots. After planting, trim existing shoots back to one bud and in January treat the bush to a high-nitrogen feed. A good mulch on top of damp, weed-free ground should ensure you can start picking in July.

COLOUR CHOICES

Mark's Dad had to take out a second mortgage to cope with his Mum's love of redcurrants. Of all the berries and currants these are the most acquired of tastes, as well as the most expensive, and often the hardest to find in the shops. (White currants are a variation on the same theme.)

Plant as for blackcurrants but not as deep, as these currants fruit on branches off the main stems, so they don't need to keep producing new ones. Add a good helping of potash (use the bonfire ashes) when planting, and again in January, and mulch with grass cuttings in spring.

The early variety Jonkeer van Tets and the mid season Laxton's No1 are both good croppers, as is White Versailles.

Have a look at IDEA 18, *Blow the raspberries*, to help you grow all the rest of the ingredients for a summer pudding.

Try another idea...

HARD AND HAIRY

The gooseberry can be one of the ultimate tastes in the garden. Pick the right one from the bush that is slightly softer, and slightly browner than other berries, and your taste buds will be dancing. Get it wrong, however, and they'll be quivering as the tart juices attack your palate.

These fruits are fully self-fertile, hardy and prolific. They come in shades of red, white, green or yellow and can be eaten raw from the bush, or used in sorbets, pies and crumbles, and to flavour savoury sauces.

The planting and care is similar to redcurrants. Get them in the ground between November and February, remove the lower branches to a height of 15cm – this makes picking easier and less painful – and cut back main stems by half. To create an open, airy bush you can also cut down the growth in the centre to just one bud,

Defining idea...

'*These imaginary pictures were of different kinds according to the advertisements which he came across, but for some reason in every one of them he had always to have gooseberries. He could not imagine a homestead, he could not picture an idyllic nook, without gooseberries.*'
From *Gooseberries* by ANTON CHEKHOV

which should help prevent mildew, a common problem with gooseberries. Keep a lookout too for gooseberry saw fly and pick off any tiny larvae as soon as you spot them, before they strip the bush of leaves.

You can start picking at the end of May/early June, but to get both cooking and dessert fruit from the same bush, simply pick alternate berries, leaving the rest of the fruit to ripen like grapes. Varieties such as 'Early sulphur' and the yellow-fruited 'Leveller' have good flavour cooked or eaten raw. 'White Lion' has large whitish fruit, while for the novelty of a red gooseberry, try 'Pax'.

PRUNING FOR PRODUCTION

On the bush form of blackcurrants prune out about a third of the plant to ground level each year to encourage new stems. It's easiest to do this at the same time as picking, so you can simply take the pruned branches into the kitchen and remove the fruit.

Red and white currants, and gooseberries, need both summer and winter pruning. In summer tidy up the plant, trimming side shoots to four or five leaves and taking out any cross shoots. In winter take the side shoots back to two buds and cut the lead shoots back by half.

Q   To save space can I grow my fruit bushes against the wall?

A   *Gooseberries and red and white currants can be trained against a fence or wall on wires as 'fans' with their stems spread out, or on a single upright stem as a 'cordon'. Trained fruit is easy to prune, protect and pick. Leave 5cm at least between the plant and its support, and refer to a pruning book to find out how to encourage a good crop.*

Q   Having planted, pruned and pampered my currants do I need to protect the fruit from the birds?

A   *Unless netted, your precious currants and any gooseberries left to ripen on the bush will be devoured by the birds. Place four canes, with a small plant pot on top, around each plant. Spread a net over the top and secure at the bottom with bricks so no feathered or other 'friends' can creep inside.*

How did
it go?

The end...

Or is it a new beginning? We hope that this book has inspired you to transform your garden. Maybe you're trying some plant varieties you hadn't heard of before, or started a pond or a wildlife garden. When your friends visit we hope they're knocked sideways by your inspired use of shades and textures. Let us know if that's the case. We'd like to be as amazed and impressed as they are.

So tell us how you got on. What did it for you – what helped you to turn that old bed into something the Chelsea Flower Show would be proud of? Maybe you've got some tips of your own you want to share (see next page if so). And if you liked this book you may find we have even more brilliant ideas that could change other areas of your life for the better.

You'll find the Infinite Ideas crew waiting for you online at www.infideas.com.

Or if you prefer to write, then send your letters to:
Create your dream garden
The Infinite Ideas Company Ltd
36 St Giles, Oxford OX1 3LD, United Kingdom

We want to know what you think, because we're all working on making our lives better too. Give us your feedback and you could win a copy of another *52 Brilliant Ideas* book of your choice. Or maybe get a crack at writing your own.

Good luck. Be brilliant.

Offer one

CASH IN YOUR IDEAS

We hope you enjoy this book. We hope it inspires, amuses, educates and entertains you. But we don't assume that you're a novice, or that this is the first book that you've bought on the subject. You've got ideas of your own. Maybe our authors have missed an idea that you use successfully. If so, why not send it to info@infideas.com, and if we like it we'll post it on our bulletin board. Better still, if your idea makes it into print we'll send you £50 and you'll be fully credited so that everyone knows you've had another Brilliant Idea.

Offer two

HOW COULD YOU REFUSE?

Amazing discounts on bulk quantities of Infinite Ideas books are available to corporations, professional associations and other organizations.

For details call us on:
+44 (0)1865 514888
or e-mail: info@infideas.com

Where it's at...